Christianity for Hindus

Christianity for Hindus

Arvind Sharma

D.K. Printworld (P) Ltd.
New Delhi

Cataloging in Publication Data — DK

[Courtesy: D.K. Agencies (P) Ltd. <docinfo@dkagencies.com>]

Sharma, Arvind, 1940-

Christianity for Hindus / Arvind Sharma.

p. cm.

Includes bibliographical references.

ISBN 13: 9788124605400

ISBN 10: 8124605408

1. Christianity and other religions – Hinduism.
2. Hinduism – Relations – Christianity. I. Title.

DDC 261.245 22

First published in India, 2010

ISBN 13: 978-81-246-0540-0 (Pb) ISBN 10: 81-246-0540-8

Published and printed by:

D.K. Printworld (P) Ltd.

Regd. office : *'Srikunj,'* F-52, Bali Nagar

Ramesh Nagar Metro Station

New Delhi – 110 015

Phones : (011) 2545 3975; 2546 6019; *Fax* : (011) 2546 5926

E-mail: indology@dkprintworld.com

Web: www.dkprintworld.com

Preface

INDIA is a religiously plural country. Religious plurality is a good thing, especially if accompanied by religious tolerance. Religious tolerance is also a good thing but at times it can degenerate into religious complacency, or worse, indifference, and finally into ignorance, as we lose all interest in knowing about the faith of our neighbour, which may be a matter of life and death for him or her. Or even more important than that.

Such ignorance is not bliss, although those who favour a throughly secular dispensation may be inclined to think so. On the contrary, an acquaintance with the fundamentals of world's religions is highly desirable, and may even be necessary in the modern world. More problems are caused by not knowing about other religions than by knowing about them, warts and all. For instance, those who tend to view Christianity as a predatory religion, bent on preying on the flock of other religions, may be pleasantly surprised to learn, upon reading the last chapter, that not all Christians think that way.

Would the Mutineers, upon taking Delhi in 1857, have killed every Christian there — European and Indian — if they knew not what they but what Christianity stood for?

Contents

1

Why Study Christianity?

Why should a Hindu study Christianity?

MANY reasons could be adduced. There is a good statistical reason to begin with. About 33.6 per cent of the world, or one out of every three persons on the surface of the globe, is a Christian.[1]

In this age of globalization, when the whole world is becoming a global village, it is like getting to know one's neighbour.

It is not only as a citizen of the world that one needs to understand Christianity. One also needs to understand it as a religion of India. We associate Christianity with Rome but if the Christian accounts regarding St Thomas are to be believed, Christianity may have reached India before it reached Rome. According to the story of St Thomas, Christianity was preached in India as early as "middle of the first century CE"[2] while St Paul was martyred in Rome

---

1. Mary Pat Fischer, *Living Religions* (3rd edn.) (Upper Saddle River, N.J.: Prentice Hall, 1997), p. 423.

2. D.C. Sircar, "The Yavanas," in R.C. Majumdar, ed., *The Age of Imperial Unity* (Bombay: Bharatiya Vidya Bhavan, 1968), p. 130.

c. CE 65.[3] The legend of Apostle Thomas cannot be traced prior to the third century CE.[4] But even so there is little doubt about a Christian presence in India from that century onwards, if not earlier.[5] According to one view, the early Christians who came to India were fleeing from persecution in Persia, and found safe heaven here the way the Jews had after the destruction of the Second Temple in CE 70. Moreover, close to 3 per cent of India's population identifies itself as Christian in the Indian census.

Thus one needs to know about Christianity both as a citizen of the world and as a citizen of India. Yet another reason why one might wish to know more about Christianity flows from the fact that it is part and parcel of Western culture which now dominates the world. Just recall what you did at Christmas last year and you will know what I am saying. Christianity did not originate in Europe (it actually originated in Asia!) but it was in Europe that it gained a foothold during the Roman Empire and then grew from strength to strength. Many modern presidents of the USA have openly drawn spiritual strength from Christianity: Jimmy Carter, Ronald Regan, George Bush and now Barack Obama to name only four. These are some good secular reasons for gaining an understanding of Christianity.

But there are good religious reasons also for wishing to know more about Christianity. Mahatma Gandhi is said to

---

3. Willard G. Oxtoby, "The Christian Tradition", in Willard G. Oxtoby, ed., *World Religions: Western Traditions* (Toronto: Oxford University Press, 1996), p. 214.

4. R.C. Majumdar, ed., *The Age of Imperial Unity* (Bombay: Bharatiya Vidya Bhavan, 1968), p. 628.

5. Ibid.

have read more than 80 books on Christianity and in fact it can be said that his coupling of truth and non-violence — *satya* and *ahiṁsā* — in personal and public life, may have been anticipated, if it was not inspired, by the example of Jesus Christ. No representation depicts the teaching of Christianity more powerfully than the figure of Christ on the cross. Now Jesus Christ stood by the truth that he was the Messiah, the saviour-figure the people of his time were expecting. There is the "undeniable fact that he was executed as a pretender to the messiahship (*Mark* XV, 2, 9, 26), which must have involved on his part the acknowledgement of some sort of Messianic claim. Whether or not, therefore, we accept as authentic Jesus, affirmative reply to the high priest's question at his trial: 'Art thou Christ, the son of the blessed?' (*Mark* XIV, 61) we are bound to recognize that in some sense, Jesus did interpret his mission in terms of the Messiah."[6] It is worth pointing out that Jesus could have saved himself by simply denying that he was the Messiah, a simple "lie" would have gotten him not only off the hook but off the cross, but he didn't. That is how he stood for truth.

And how did he uphold non-violence? One could simply say that he did so by allowing himself to be crucified. He *gave* his life for his claim, he did not *take* a life to prove his claim. But there is a deeper background to it. Just as the Indians were smarting under British rule in the early part of the twentieth century, the Jews had been smarting under Roman rule in the early part of the Christian era. And just

6. J.G. Davies, "Christianity: The Early Church", in R.C. Zaehner, ed., *The Concise Encyclopedia of Living Faiths* (Boston: Beacon Press, 1967), p. 52.

as some Indians supported the British and some opposed them, and some were indifferent to them, and those who opposed them wanted to do so either violently or non-violently, the Jews under Roman rule were caught up in a similar situation represented by the four parties in Jesus' time. The Essenes had withdrawn into a community life of "disciplined piety," as in an *āśrama*. One might wish to think of Sri Aurobindo retiring to Pondicherry in this context. The Sadducees had accepted Roman rule and supported it like the millions of Indians serving under the British. The Pharisees sought to be as orthodox as possible to preserve the tradition, and may be compared to the Sanātanīs in India. Alongside the Essenes, the Sadducees and the Pharisees were also the Zealots, who wanted to expel the Romans by force, just as the terrorists wanted to drive the British away by force. Just like Gandhi, "into this political cauldron Jesus introduced a fifth option. Unlike the Sadducees, he wanted change. Unlike the Essenes, he stayed in the world. Unlike the advocates of military option, he extolled peacemakers and urged that even enemies be loved."[7] And just as Mahatma Gandhi emphasized Hinduism's charity at the expense, if necessary, of ritual purity, it "was the Pharisees that Jesus stood closest to. . . . The Pharisees stressed Yahweh's holiness, while Jesus stressed Yahweh's compassion."[8]

Jesus Christ thus provides an interesting parallel to Mahatma Gandhi. Both were prepared to stand by their truth and die for it, but not to kill for it.

---

7. Huston Smith, *The World's Religions* (San Francisco: Harper, 1991), p. 321.

8. Ibid.

There are thus good moral and spiritual reasons for Hindus to take note of Christianity. Perhaps Hindus don't realize how close they are to Christians in this respect. The Gandhian legacy is not the only basis for making such a statement. Sometimes things we do not know about ourselves are obvious to outsiders. This is what the Muslim savant, Al-Biruni (973-1048), whom one scholar has even described as "one of the greatest scholars ever,"[9] wrote in the eleventh century:

> In this regard the manners and customs of the Hindus resemble those of the Christians, for they are, like those of the latter, based on the principles of virtue and abstinence from wickedness, such as never to kill under any circumstance whatsoever, to give to him who has stripped you of your coat also your shirt, to offer to him who has beaten your cheek the other cheek also, to bless your enemy and to pray for him. Upon my life, this is a noble philosophy; but the people of this world are not all philosophers. Most of them are ignorant and erring, who cannot be kept on the straight road save by the sword and the whip. And, indeed, ever since Constantine the Victorious became a Christian, both sword and whip have ever been employed, for without them it would be impossible to rule.[10]

In other words, a famous medieval Muslim scholar considered Hindu morality identical with the best of Christian morality!

---

9. Wilhelm Halbfass, *India and Europe: An Essay in Understanding* (Albany, N.Y.: State University of New York Press, 1988), p. 25.
10. Edward C. Sachau, tr., *Alberuni's India* (London: Kegan Paul, Trench, Trübner & Co., 1914), vol. II, p. 161.

2

Who is Jesus Christ?

CHRISTIANITY is a historical religion. It is important for a Hindu to realize this because Hinduism is not a "historical" religion in the sense Christianity is. Of course, in one sense, Hinduism is also a historical religion, inasmuch as it possesses a history. But what is at issue becomes apparent when we ask the question: When did Hinduism begin?

There is no identifiable point in time when Hinduism can be said to have begun because Hinduism has no historical founder, certainly not in the singular should it be argued that the *ṛṣis* to whom the Vedas were revealed were in some sense its founders. But the Vedas themselves are said to be revealed at the beginning of each cycle, and this series of cycles is considered beginningless, *anādi*. It is thus difficult to provide Hinduism, in its own self-understanding, with a temporal footing and in its modern understanding, as a religious tradition, with a historical footing.

By contrast, Christianity is traced back to a person, who was "a Jewish carpenter who, as has often been pointed out, was born in a stable, was executed as a criminal at the age of thirty-three, never travelled more than 90 miles from his birthplace, owned nothing, attended no college, marshalled no army and instead of producing books did his only writing in the sand. Nevertheless, his birthday is kept across the world and his death day sets a gallows against almost every skyline. Who was he?"[1]

At one level the answer can be provided with arid brevity as follows:

> He was born in Palestine during the reign of Herod the Great, probably around 4 BCE — our reckoning of the centuries that purports to date from his birth is almost certainly off by several years. He grew up in or near Nazareth, presumably after the fashion of other normal Jews of the time. He was baptized by John, a dedicated prophet who was electrifying the region with his proclamation of God's coming judgement. In his early thirties he had a teaching-healing career, which lasted between one and three years and was focused largely in Galilee. In time he incurred the hostility of some of his own compatriots and the suspicion of Rome, which led to his crucifixion on the outskirts of Jerusalem. From these facts that fix the framework of Jesus' life, we turn to the life that was lived within that framework.[2]

In order to get a fuller answer to the question one has to turn to the text in which this life is embedded, namely the Bible. And when we turn to the Bible we find that Jesus Christ arrives on the scene at the end of a long process, which began with creation itself. The Hindu must once again realize that, as opposed to the numerous times the universe comes into being according to mainline Hindu thought, this universe is created only once by God according to Christianity.

---

1. Huston Smith, op. cit., pp. 317-18.
2. Ibid., p. 318.

So the universe is created by God, as described in the opening chapter of the Bible called the Genesis, according to which God creates heaven and earth, and a garden called Eden, and man "in his own image" (*Genesis* I, 27). However, after a period of paradisiacal existence, man is expelled from heaven for rebelling against God and soon "all flesh had corrupted his way upon the earth" (*Genesis* VI, 12). Things get so bad that God plans to wipe everything out with a flood but spares Noah, so that life is renewed,[3] but the problem of corruption persists. "God's method of dealing with this situation was to choose one man, Abraham, out of all the fallen mass of mankind, whose descendants were to form a nucleus of faithful people, and to be both the recipients of the divine blessing and the source of its mediation to all men."[4] Most scholars place Abraham *c.* 1800 BCE.

The Bible records the history of his descendants, first in Canaan (the region where the state of Israel now exists), and then in Egypt, where they ultimately end up as slaves. They are led to freedom by Moses out of Egypt and back to Canaan. Moses, under divine inspiration, asks the Egyptian Pharaoh to free "his" people. At first the Pharaoh refuses, but changes his mind when his land is afflicted by various

---

3. The account of Noah's flood is passed over, as it is not of direct relevance, but it has a Hindu parallel in the account of the incarnation of Viṣṇu as a fish which saves Manu. Elements of the account are as old as the *Śatapatha Brāhmaṇa*, see Louis Renou, ed., *Hinduism* (New York: George Braziller, 1962), pp. 84-85.

4. J.G. Davies, op. cit., p. 51.

plagues, and lets the Hebrews go. He changes his mind again but the Hebrews make a marvellous escape. According to most scholars these events occurred *c.* 1250 BCE during the reign of the Pharaoh, Ramses II. Moses is as important a figure in the history of the descendants of Abraham as Abraham himself, and the two together are foundational to Judaism — the first as the progenitor and the second as the organizer. Under him the Hebrews enter into a covenant with God, who is called Yahweh (a name whose utterance is considered sacrilegious by the orthodox). The famous Ten Commandments are said to have been handed by God to Moses on Mount Sinai, where Moses encountered God as a burning bush, which, although in flames, was not reduced to ashes.

The people prosper after the return to the "promised land" and Jewish kingdom reaches its peak under David and Solomon. But the kingdom breaks up, after Solomon's death around 921 BCE, into Judah and Israel, and gets caught up in turmoil of the political currents of the Middle-East, as much in turmoil then as now. Israel, the kingdom of the northern tribes, falls to an Assyrian invasion in 722 BCE while Judah falls to a Babylonian invasion in 586 BCE and the Hebrews are sent in exile to Babylon. These political reversals were God's punishment of his people for straying from the path he had laid out for them according to Jewish self-understanding, about which their own prophets periodically warned them.

> Despite the warnings of the prophets, the Israelites did not persevere in the way of righteousness and so they were brought to the suffering of the Exile in Babylonia. Then, in penitence, hope revived and they looked forward to a

> restoration when the powers of evil should be overthrown, when God's Kingdom or rule should be set up, exercised either directly or through his promised Messiah, and a New Covenant should be established (*Jeremiah* XXXI, 31). Neither the events immediately succeeding the return from Babylon nor the short-lived independence of the Jews under the Maccabean house satisfied this hope, as successive foreign powers held them in submission, from the Persians in the sixth century BCE to the Romans in the latter half of the first. But the hope did not die, and when St Luke, in the second chapter of his Gospel, referred to Simeon as a man "looking for the consolation of Israel," he was describing an attitude typical of the majority of the Jews of his day. The New Testament affirmation — and it is this that constituted in the understanding of its first proclaimers as the Gospel or Good News — is to the effect that this hope was now in process of fulfilment through the mission of Jesus of Nazareth.[5]

That is why we find people asking Jesus, when he appeared on the scene, whether he was the Messiah. We need to deal with two questions in this respect: whether he was the Messiah, and if so, what kind of a Messiah.

The question whether he was the Messiah or not is important, for it is the answer to this question which today divides Christianity from Judaism, although the answer would have been more equivocal in Jesus' own time. In some contexts, according to the Biblical record, Jesus is not forthcoming on the point, as when the demoniacs identify him as such (*Mark* I, 25; III, 11-12) or even in the case of his disciple Peter (*Mark* VIII, 29-30). However, he does answer in the affirmative when his life hangs in balance on the

5. J.G. Davies, op. cit., p. 51.

right answer, when questioned by the high priest at the trial (*Mark* XIV, 61) and is executed as "a pretender to Messiahship (*Mark* XV, 2, 9, 26)." How is this ambiguity to be explained?

One possible explanation connects the question of whether he was the Messiah with the question of what kind of a Messiah was he going to be. The popular view was that the Messiah would be a royal figure from the line of David (to which Jesus indeed belonged). But his own conception of Messiahship could have been rather different, in fact, so different, that it made Jesus' self-identification with the Messiah problematical. This is one view.

Another explanation follows a different tack and is best understood in terms of the difference between President and the President-elect on the American political scene.

> If this be applied to Jesus, it means that during his ministry he is Messiah designate; only after he has accomplished his mission is he to be enthroned as Messiah. Alternatively it may be said that Jesus is only the Saviour when he has completed his work of salvation which involved not just his birth, but his death, resurrection and ascension. Here then is the probable reason for Jesus' refusal to declare himself, until his work was complete.[6]

It is important for Hindus to understand Jesus' role as the Messiah because this imparts special significance to his resurrection — that is, that he is found visibly (but somewhat intangibly) alive even after his death and burial. Dead people coming back to life is of course highly unusual but not unknown in either Christian or Hindu literature. Jesus himself brought Lazarus back to life according to the Biblical

6. J.G. Davies, op. cit., pp. 52-53.

accounts, so what's so special about the same happening to Jesus? The answer lies in the fact the Jesus was the Messiah who had *foretold* that "the Son of Man must suffer many things . . . be killed . . . and . . . rise again" (*Mark* VIII, 31). Śrī Kṛṣṇa brought Parīkṣit back to life too, to continue the royal line, but here again there is no parallel Messianic context.

The fact that Jesus rose from the dead is very important — in many ways. Many people in the ancient world had claimed to be the son of God, or even God, but none of their claims survived their death. Whether Jesus himself claimed to be the son of God, or whether this claim is really a claim made by the Church, is not entirely clear. Jesus clearly saw himself as standing in a special filial relationship with God (*Matthew* XI, 27; *Luke* X, 22) but whether he looked upon himself as the son of God, as he is understood in the doctrine of the trinity (to be explained later), is uncertain. Some scholars have argued that *he* looked upon *himself* as an eschatological prophet and not as the "son of God" in the orthodox sense and that this self-understanding of his may be better reflected in Islam and even Judaism. But one can see how, if one died claiming to be the son of God in some sense, and returned from the dead, it would be hard to avoid the conclusion that he was the son of God in every sense. Now we are in a position to grasp the significance of the following passage:

> Faith in Jesus' resurrection produced the Church and its Christology. To grasp the power of the belief, we must see that it did not merely concern the fate of a worthy man. Its claim extended ultimately to the status of goodness in the universe, contending that it was all-powerful. If Golgotha's

> cross had been the end, the goodness Jesus embodied would have been beautiful, but how significant? A fragile blossom afloat on a torrential stream, soon to be dashed — how relevant is goodness if it has no purchase on reality, no power at its disposal? The resurrection reversed the cosmic position in which the cross had placed Jesus' goodness. Instead of being fragile, the compassion the disciples had encountered in him was powerful; victorious over everything, even the seeming end of everything, death itself. "Grave, where is your victory? Death, where is your sting?"[7]

The miracles performed by Jesus Christ also assume their full significance in the context of the Messiahship of Jesus. There is a tendency on the part of the Hindus to look upon the miracles of Jesus as spiritual razzle dazzle, or "special effects" to which as a culture they are quite used. Thus when Christian missionaries tried to impress them with the miracles of Jesus early in the nineteenth century, the Hindus "pointed out that the raising of Lazarus from the dead was unworthy of remark; their own religion had many more interesting and astonishing miracles than this; and any true *yogī* could perform miracles today, while those of Christianity were apparently finished."[8] When Raja Rammohun Roy published his own version of the *New Testament* he excluded miracles from it because the "miraculous relations" found therein "are much less wonderful than the fabricated tales handed down to the natives of Asia, and consequently would be apt at best to carry little weight with them."[9] The point to note here is

7. Huston Smith, op. cit., p. 330.
8. Will Durant, *Our Oriental Heritage* (New York: Simon and Schuster, 1954), p. 615.
9. Cited, in Stephen Hay, ed., *Sources of Indian Tradition* (2nd edn.) (New York: Columbia University Press, 1988), vol. II, p. 25.

that the miracles of Jesus are the harbinger of the new age of God's rule on earth, and they "can no longer be discarded, as in the hey-day of liberal theology, as unnecessary embellishments of the simple Gospel record; rather they are to be understood as signs that the age of salvation is dawning."[10]

The enormous significance of the Messiah concept in and around the time of Jesus is confirmed by the so-called Dead Sea Scrolls which were discovered hidden in jars by a shepherd in 1947 near the Dead Sea at Qumran and hence came to be known as they are. The texts reveal that there were, around this period, expectations of a royal Messiah, a priestly Messiah, and a Messiah who would combine these roles.[11]

---

10. J.G. Davies, op. cit., p. 52.

11. See Gerbern S. Oegema, *The Anointed and His People* (Sheffield: Sheffield Academic Press, 1998).

3

Doctrines of the Church

I

THE resurrection event rejuvenated the disciples of Jesus Christ, who were at first inclined to dismiss the report of his first sighting by Mary Magdalene. Thus the first witness to the event of the resurrection was apparently a woman. Similarly, the first person to become a Muslim in the world was also arguably a woman — the Prophet's own wife, Khadījah. These facts were well known; the growing feminist awareness of our times helps to highlight them.

The resurrection, however, was really an earnest to the Second Coming, when Jesus Christ will return in all his glory and establish the rule of God on earth. There was however an element of ambiguity in the situation: Jesus Christ did foretell his return in this manner but did not provide a specific time for it. Now as the Christian community waited for his return, the general prophecy of his return gradually got converted into one of early return. Four main factors could have operated to transform a prophecy of a return into a prophecy of an *immediate* return. These are:

(i) the certainty, characteristic of apocalyptic literature, that what is predicted is close at hand: "the time will come and will not tarry" (*Apocalypse of Baruch*, XX, 6); "my salvation has truly drawn nigh, and it is no longer distant as formerly" (ibid. XXIII, 7; cf. *Revelation* I, I);

(ii) the influence of Old Testament prophecy with its eager expectancy;

(iii) the rapid progress of the Gospel, which would suggest a speedy preparation of mankind for the Second Coming;

(iv) the outbreak of persecution, which would lead to a quickened faith in divine vindication, and in the revelation of Christ in glory to judge and punish the persecutors.[1]

In the meantime, Christianity was gaining converts in the Roman Empire, through a process we would today call networking,[2] against heavy odds. There were persecutions but in Tertullian's famous phrase: "The blood of the martyr is the seed of the Church" and the seed sprouted in the early years of the fourth century CE when Constantine emblazoned the shields of the soldiers with the Christian cross after a vision and went on to win a key battle.[3] In 313, the Christians were given freedom to practise their religion and under Theodosius 1 (r. 379-95) the empire became a Christian state.[4]

---

1. J.G. Davies, op. cit., p. 55.
2. See Rodney Stark, *The Rise of Christianity* (Harper San-Francisco, 1997).
3. Willard G. Oxtoby, ed., *World Religions: Western Traditions* (Toronto: Oxford University Press, 1996) p. 226.
4. Ibid., p. 227.

But before this could happen, the "right teaching" of Christianity had to be established, as this had become a matter of controversy. So Constantine, as he took hold of the empire, also found himself concerned with the state of the Church. Constantine called all the bishops to meet at Nicaea in 325 to sort out the matter and the Council came up with what has since been called the Nicene Creed, which was ratified in its present form in 381. It runs as follows:

> We believe in one God, the Father almighty, maker of heaven and earth, and of all things visible and invisible; and in one Lord Jesus Christ, the only-begotten Son of God, begotten of the Father before all worlds, God of God, light of light, very God of very God, begotten not made, being of one substance with the Father, by whom all things were made, who for us men and for our salvation came down from heaven, and was incarnate by the Holy Spirit of the Virgin Mary, and was made man, and was crucified for us under Pontius Pilate. He suffered and was buried, and the third day he rose again according to the scriptures, and ascended into heaven, and sits on the right hand of the Father, and he shall come again with glory to judge both the living and the dead; whose kingdom shall have no end. And we believe in the Holy Spirit, the Lord and giver of life, who proceeds from the Father (and the Son), who with the Father and Son together is worshipped and glorified, who spoke by the prophets. And we believe in one holy catholic and apostolic church. We acknowledge one baptism for the remission of sins. And we look for the resurrection of the dead, and the life of the world to come.[5]

II

This creedal formulation just cited is likely to leave a Hindu

5. Cited in Willard G. Oxtoby, op. cit., pp. 231-32.

unmoved not merely on account of the *contents* which may seem foreign to him but on account of the *form* in which they are cast, namely, that of a creed whose acceptance or rejection decides whether one is a Christian or not. From a Hindu perspective, practice tends to be more important than dogma; how you behave is more important than what you believe in. In the case of Christianity, while conduct is not neglected, *belief* in a creed is emphasized to an extent a Hindu may find difficult to relate to. A comparative religionist, Willard Oxtoby, offers a helpful reflection on this point:

> Very early in the history of Christianity, the Church arrived at formulations of the content of its faith. Especially before Constantine, such statements served as tests of the seriousness and commitment of individuals joining the movement. The use of creeds (the term is from the Latin for belief) has had a lasting influence on Christian understanding of themselves and of others. Christians have defined themselves as people who believe such-and-such about Jesus or about God and the world, and — often misleadingly — they have expected other traditions to be formulated in terms of belief as well.[6]

So one step towards a better understanding of Christianity consists of realizing that, within it, statements of belief count in a way they might not in the case of Indic religions.

One may now select three items of such beliefs from the Nicene Creed for further exploration.

Incarnation

Incarnation is of course a doctrine Hindus are not

---

6. Cited in Willard G. Oxtoby, op. cit., p. 231.

unfamiliar with. Any presentation of Hinduism worth its name speaks of the ten incarnations of Viṣṇu (*daśāvatāra*).[7] And perhaps one of the best known and oft quoted verses of the *Bhagavad-Gītā* (IV.8) deals with Kṛṣṇa's promise that he sends himself forth age after age to save the virtuous and eradicate the wicked.

There is however a difference on the point of the *number* of incarnations and the *nature* of incarnation in Christian and Hindu thought. Hindu thought admits of numerous incarnations. The list of ten itself contains variant readings and the ten are in any case meant to be illustrative rather than exhaustive. For Christianity, however, Jesus Christ is the one and only incarnation of God. One might add, with philosophical circumspection, that within Christianity "there is a longstanding distinction between the metaphysical attributes of God (aseity, eternity, infinity, etc.) and God's moral attributes (goodness, love, wisdom, etc.). The doctrine of incarnation involves the claim that moral (but not the metaphysical) attributes of God have been embodied, so far as this is possible, in a finite human life, namely that of Jesus."[8]

Or as K.M. Sen puts it:

> Unlike Christianity which accepts only one unique Divine Incarnation in Jesus Christ, Hindus accept many

7. A.L. Basham, *The Wonder That Was India* (New Delhi: Rupa & Co., 1999), pp. 301-07; Arvind Sharma, *Classical Hindu Thought: An Introduction* (New Delhi: Oxford University Press, 2001), pp. 84-86.
8. John H. Hick, *Philosophy of Religion* (4th edn.) (Englewood Cliffs, New Jersey: Prentice Hall, 1990), p. 88.

> incarnations of God. In the *Bhagavad-Gītā* the lord says: "For whensoever the law fails and lawlessness uprises, then do I bring myself to bodied birth. To guard righteousness, to destroy evil-doers, to establish the law, I come into birth age after age" (fourth lesson, verses 7 and 8). While some Hindus take the doctrine literally and accept figures like Rāma, Kṛṣṇa, and Buddha as actual incarnations, others prefer to treat is as a useful myth.[9]

It wouldn't do, however, to treat incarnation as a useful myth in Christianity. In fact, the Hindu theology of incarnation, in a sense, makes it easier to treat incarnation as a myth should one want to, although it does not say that incarnation is a myth. What it does say is that God appears to act like a human being *without* the implication that God actually becomes a human being like you and me. The point became an important one in the history of Christianity, and raised the question that if it was "declared to be orthodoxy [that] the eternal son is coequal with the father, then how does the eternal divinity of Jesus relate to his historical humanity?"[10] The following "three principal options" emerged in the context:

(1) Two separate persons, one divine, one human;

(2) One person with only a divine nature;

(3) One person but with *both* a divine nature and a human nature.[11]

This third position was accepted as the orthodox position by the Greek- and Latin-speaking churches.

---

9. K.M. Sen, *Hinduism* (Harmondsworth: Penguin, 1961), p. 73 n. 1.
10. Willard Oxtoby, op. cit., p. 234.
11. Ibid.

The issue is important from both an epistemological and an ontological point of view. Huston Smith notes:

> Holding as it does that in Christ God assumed a human body, it affirms that Christ was God-Man; simultaneously both fully God and fully man. To say that such a contention is paradoxical seems a charitable way to put the matter — it looks more like a blatant contradiction. If the doctrine held that Christ was half human and half divine, or that he was divine in certain respects while being human in others, our minds would not balk. But such concessions are precisely what the Creeds refuse to grant. In the words of the Creed of Chalcedon, Jesus Christ was "at once complete in Godhead and complete in manhood, truly God and truly man . . . of one essence with the Father as regards his Godhead, and at the same time of one essence with us as regards his manhood, in all respects like us, apart from sin."
>
> The Church has always admitted that such assertions are opaque; the question is whether this is the last word on the matter. Actually, we can ask the same questions of science. The anomalies of frontier physics provoked Haldane to his famous mutterance that "the universe is not only queerer than we suppose, but queerer than we *can* suppose." In more than one field, it appears, reality can be too strange for logic to comprehend. And where logic and evidence clash, it seems prudent to stick with evidence, for this holds the prospect of leading to a wider logic, whereas the opposite approach closes the door to discovery.[12]

The ontological point has to do with the following consideration. In the world in which Christianity came into being "the dividing line between the human and the divine was perforated to the point that even emperors routinely

---

12. Huston Smith, op. cit., p. 340.

claimed to be divine."[13] Indic civilization presents a parallel case:

> Divinity was cheap in ancient India. Every brāhmaṇa was in a sense a god, as were ascetics with a reputation for sanctity. Householders sponsoring and financing sacrifices were in theory raised to divinity, at least for the duration of the ceremony, while even sticks and stones might be alive with inherent godhead.[14]

So what sets the Christian message apart? From the Christian point of view "the incarnation claimed that there was something newsworthy in the Christian message; namely, its proclamation of the kind of God that God was, as demonstrated by the God's willingness to assume a human life of the form that Jesus exemplified. That willingness, together with the character of Jesus' life, added up to a different understanding of divinity than the Mediterranean world had known. In the Christian view God was concerned about humanity; concerned enough to suffer in its behalf. This was unheard of, to the point that the reaction to it was disbelief followed by alarm."[15] There are holy figures in Hinduism and Buddhism who are willing to suffer for others, of which the *bodhisattva* is a major example. But Buddhism is non-theistic, so back to Hinduism. There are figures not only like King Vipaścit[16] but ordinary

---

13. Huston Smith, op. cit.
14. A.L. Basham, op. cit., p. 86.
15. Huston Smith, op. cit., p. 342.
16. Louis Renou, ed., *Hinduism* (New York : George Braziller, 1962), pp. 164-67.

brāhmaṇa boys willing to suffer for others,[17] but what about God? God Śiva drank poison on behalf of creation but the doctrine of incarnation never quite gained the foothold in Śaivism as it did in Vaiṣṇavism.

The incarnation of Jesus thus presents a great opportunity and an issue for Hindu students of religion. The opportunity consists of the emphasis it lays on the humanity of Jesus.

> And because in the Church's experience it was Jesus' full humanity that was in danger of slipping from their grasp, so rapidly was his divinity moving to the fore, it was that humanity that the Church's first Creed set out to affirm.
>
> *I believe in God the Father Almighty,*
> *Maker of heaven and earth;*
> *and in Jesus Christ our Lord,*
> *who was* conceived *by the Holy Ghost,*
> born *of the Virgin Mary,*
> suffered *under Pontius Pilate,*
> *was* crucified, died, *and* buried. . . .
>
> How casually this Apostles' Creed touches on Christ's divinity! As early as the second century this point no longer had to be argued; it was assumed. The burden of the Apostles' Creed, carried by the words we have Romanized, was to insist that Christ was man as well. He *really was* born, it says; he really suffered, he really died and was buried. These incidents were not just make-believe, a sequence through which God merely feigned to brush with the human estate; that notion was later targeted as the Docetic Heresy. Christ endured these experiences as fully as we do. He was "truly man."[18]

---

17. J.A.B. van Buitenen, *Tales of Ancient India* (Chicago: The University of Chicago Press, 1959), pp. 43-51.

18. Huston Smith, op. cit., p. 342.

Buddhism provides an interesting parallel. It has been pointed out that in a land where the tendency to deify is very strong, it is to the credit of the Theravāda Buddhism that it has retained the human conception of the Buddha for so long. The formula that one finds most often in the Pāli scriptures reads as follows:

> The Blessed One is an *arhat*, a fully awakened one, endowed with knowledge and good conduct, happy, a knower of the world, unsurpassed leader able to control men, teacher of men and gods, the awakened, the blessed.

The humanity of the Buddha is also expressed by a Theravāda monk, arguing against the encroachment of what he considered to be heretical views:

> Was he not born at Lumbinī, superenlightened under the *bodhi* tree? Was not the Norm-wheel set rolling by him at Benares? . . . Did he not complete existence at Kuśinārā?[19]

A problem arises when one tries to identify examples from Hinduism which may parallel those of Jesus Christ: How could Jesus be human if he was divinely conceived? Mahatma Gandhi gives expression to the predicament as follows:

> If you read the Qur'ān, you must read it with the eye of the Muslim; if you read the Bible, you must read it with the eye of the Christian; if you read the *Gītā*, you must read it with the eye of a Hindu. Where is the use of scanning details and then holding up a religion to ridicule? Take the very first chapter of Genesis or of Matthew. We read a long pedigree and then at the end we are told Jesus was born of a virgin.

---

19. Kenneth K.S. Ch'en, *Buddhism: The Light of Asia* (Haupagge, N.Y.: Barrons' Educational Series, 1968), p. 63.

> You come up against a blind wall. But I must read it all with the eye of a Christian.[20]

Atonement

In order to grasp the significance of what is at stake in this doctrine, one needs to refer back to the story of creation and the expulsion of Adam from Eden for disobeying God. Things went downhill from then on. It is as if humanity had been paying the price of that sin as descendants of Adam.

> As this sin was directed against God it was of infinite proportion. Sins must be compensated for, otherwise God's justice would be compromised. An infinite sin demands infinite recompense, and this could only be effected by God's vicarious assumption of our guilt and payment of the ultimate penalty required, namely, death. God made this payment through the Person of Christ and the debt was cancelled.[21]

This has been called the legalistic interpretation of atonement.

The idea of debt (*ṛṇa*) and the paying off of that debt is not foreign to Hinduism. Every twice-born is said to be born with three debts: to the gods, sages, and the manes, and that they are discharged by offering oblations into the ritual fire, by studying the Vedas and by begetting a son (or appointing a substitute) respectively. It is the scale of the debt and the involvement of God rather than the gods which set the Christian example apart. Even the Hindu view of three debts could be extended to five debts, to match the

20. M.K. Gandhi, *Hindu Dharma* (Ahmedabad: Navajivan Press, 1958), p. 234.

21. Huston Smith, op. cit., p. 343.

five elements of the *pañca-mahāyajña* or the five sacrifices, three of which (*deva-ṛṣi-pitṛ yajña*) have been already alluded to. The other two — *mānuṣa-* and *bhūta-yajña* — consist of hospitality to human beings and the care of sub-human creatures in the form of scattering food for birds, etc. But even such an extension cannot hope to match even remotely the colossal scale of the Christian enterprise. The tradition in Tamil Nadu that once a month at Tillai (Chidambaram) Śiva performs the *tāṇḍava* dance in front of his spouse Pārvatī, and all the sins of the world committed until then are thereby destroyed, comes closer but while it contains a charismatic element it was hardly ever given a legalistic formulation.

The other understanding of atonement is moral and has to do with a person feeling trapped in a negative course of action. Paul moans his lot in the following words: "I do not do what I want, but I do the very thing I hate" (Romans 14:15) which is reminiscent of a statement in the *Mahābhārata* often attributed to Duryodhana — "I know what is right but can't do it and I know what is wrong but can't stop doing it" (*jānāmi dharmaṁ na ca me nivṛttiḥ, jānāmyadharmaṁ na ca me pravṛttiḥ*). Duryodhana however does not share the moral agony of Paul and blames it all on some "divine" force which compels him to act the way he does. Although Duryodhana's is *rhetorically* closer to Paul, Arjuna is *morally* closer to Paul in agonizing over his role in the Mahābhārata war. The interesting point is that it is only through Kṛṣṇa that Arjuna is able to overcome his predicament, just as it is only through Christ that Paul is able to resolve his. But why did both of them have to reach out beyond themselves for therapeutic intervention?

It is said to be the final step in the Alcoholics Anonymous programme that a person surrenders to a higher power. This power is represented by Kṛṣṇa and Christ in our examples. This carries one also back to the mediatorship idea — of God choosing Abraham and his descendants "to be both the recipients of the divine blessing and the source of its mediation to all men."[22] Christ is the ultimate mediator as well as the mediator of the ultimate. "If there is to be a liberation, it will have to come from without, or better, from above: a higher power. It was the Christian witness that the power that works liberation and restores the self to the ground of its being, is Christ. One could equally say that it is God, but Christians add that in this instance God's purpose was accomplished by Christ."[23]

It's as if one is caught in a treadmill and a hand has to reach out to one from out there somewhere to yank one off it.

Trinity

Another cardinal doctrine of the Christian Church is the doctrine of the trinity. How quintessentially Christian this doctrine is may be judged from the fact that both Judaism and Islam, otherwise also monotheistic and prophetic in their orientation, reject the doctrine of trinity in favour of the unity of God. And even though one would imagine that the triune description of *Brahman* in Hinduism as *saccidānanda* (*sat* + *cit* + *ānanda*) would make it more

---

22. J.G. Davies, op. cit., p. 51.
23. Huston Smith, op. cit., p. 344.

receptive to another kind of trinity, this is not how the first Hindu thinker to come in touch with Christianity in a major way, namely Raja Rammohun Roy, reacted to it. He argued for a Unitarian interpretation of Christianity and a Christian by the name of Adam found the arguments so convincing that he abandoned his Trinitarianism in favour of Unitarianism, thereby incurring the wrath of his fellow-Christians who described these happenings as the *second* fall of Adam. Raja Rammohun Roy was in fact quite unsparing in his critique of Trinitarianism, as is obvious from the following extract:

A DIALOGUE
BETWEEN
A MISSIONARY AND THREE CHINESE CONVERTS

Missionary. How many Gods are there, my brethren!

1st Convert. Three.

2nd Convert. Two.

3rd Convert. None.

Missionary. Horrid! The answers are from the Devil.

All. We know not where you got the religion which you have taught us, but thus you have taught us.

Missionary. Blasphemers!

All. We have heard you with patience nor ever thought of crying out against you, how much so ever you surprised us by your doctrine.

Missionary: (Recovering himself and addressing the 1st convert). Come, come, recollect; how can you imagine that there are three Gods?

1st Convert: You told me there was God the Father, and God the Son, and God the Holy Ghost, and by my Swanpan I find that one and one and one are three.

Missionary: O! I see your blunder. You remember but half the lesson. I told you also that these Three are One.

1st Convert: I know you did, but I thought you had forgotten yourself, and concluded that you spoke the truth at first.

Missionary: O no! You must believe not only that there are Three persons, each God, and equal in power and glory, but also, that these Three are One.

1st Convert: That is impossible. In China we do not believe contradictions.

Missionary: Brother! It is a mystery.

1st Convert: What is that, pray?

Missionary: It is — it is — I know not what to say to you, except that it is something which you cannot possibly comprehend.

1st Convert: (Smiling) And is it this that you have been sent 10,000 miles to teach?

Missionary: O the power of carnal reason! Surely, some Socinian has been doing the Devil's work in China.

But (turning to the 2nd convert), how could you imagine, there are two Gods?

2nd Convert: I thought there were many more till you came and lessened the number.

Missionary: Have I ever told you that there are two Gods? (Aside.) The stupidity of this people makes me almost despair.

2nd Convert: True, you have not said in so many words that there are two Gods, but you have said what implies it.

Missionary: Then you have been tempted to reason upon this mystery.

2nd Convert: We, Chinese, are wont to put things together and to come at truth by comparison. Thus you said there were three persons that were each perfect God, and then you said one of these persons died in one of the countries of the West, a long while ago; and I therefore concluded the present number to be two.

Missionary: Astonishing depravity! O the depths of Satan! It is in vain to reason with these poor benighted creatures. But (addressing the 3rd convert) perverse as your two brethren are, you appear worse than they: what can you possibly mean by answering that there are no Gods?

3rd Convert: I heard you talk of three, but I paid more particular attention to what you said on the point of there being only one. This I could understand; the other I could not; and as my belief never reaches above my understanding (for you know I am no learned Mandarin) I set it down in my mind that there was but one God, and that you take your name of Christian from him.

Missionary: There is something in this; but I am more and more astonished at your answer — "None."

3rd Convert: (Taking up the Swanpan.) Here is one. I remove it. There is none.

Missionary: How can this apply?

3rd Convert: Our minds are not like yours in the West, or you would not ask me. You told me again and again, that there never was but one God, that Christ was the true God, and that a nation of merchants living at the head of the Arabian gulf, put him to death upon a tree, about eighteen hundred years ago. Believing you, what other answer could I give than "None"?

Missionary: I must pray for you, for you all deny the true faith, and living and dying thus, you will without doubt perish everlastingly.

1st Convert: Cong-foo-tse, our revered master says, that bad temper always turns reasons out of doors, and that when men begin to curse, the good Spirit of the universe abandons their hearts.

2nd Convert: You must be angry with yourself and not with us, for you have been teaching us at different times doctrines as contradictory as those of Cong-foo-tse and Buddha. The immortal emperor Sinchong has said that he is not to be numbered with wise men, nor to have a name in the hall of ancestors, who undertakes a voyage without making up his mind to its purpose, and preparing himself to give a clear and kind answer to the question of a stranger.

3rd Convert: These rebukes are just: but Ter-whangtee says, in his golden words, that mirth is better than rice. You came, it seems, to bring us a new riddle: but while we thank you, we beg to inform you that Kienlong, our late celestial emperor, has supplied us with a plentiful store, much more entertaining than yours; and when you can read as well as speak our divine language, we recommend to you his delectable history of the Mantchoo Tartar, that pretended to be inspired by the Grand Lama, but could never be made to comprehend the Swanpan.[24]

The doctrine then calls for delicate treatment as essential to Christianity on the one hand yet as challenging comprehension on the other.

One might begin by trying to understand the circumstances which might have given rise to it. The

---

24. Kalidas Nag and Debajyoti Burman, eds., *The English Works of Raja Rammohun Roy* (Calcutta: Sadharan Brahmo Samaj, 1947), part IV, pp. 77-79.

Christians inherited a strict monotheism from their Jewish background. At the same time, they also encountered the divine in a very personal and powerful way in the person of Jesus Christ. Then, after the resurrection of Jesus Christ, his followers had the powerful experience of the Holy Spirit so dramatically described in the Acts (2:1-4):

> Suddenly from heaven there came a sound like the rush of a violent wind, and it filled the entire house where they were sitting. Divided tongues, as of fire, appeared among them, and a tongue rested on each of them. All of them were filled with the Holy Spirit. (Acts 2:1-4)[25]

So here was the Church having to deal with these three soul-shaking experiences and had to make sense of them within the unitary frame of monotheism. It has thus been plausibly argued that "Following its roots in the insistently monotheistic Judaic tradition, Christianity has resisted asserting a plurality of distinct gods, but it has wanted to maintain a plurality of divine 'person' or divine manifestations."[26] Such a statement is suggestive of historical reductionism but need not imply "it for the fact that the Christian community existentially encountered the divine in three ways which it knows to be one would contain its own spiritual dynamic, which would call for creedal accommodation." Thus

> The secular mind would say that the disciples first reified this experience, turning it into a thing, the Holy Spirit, and then personified that reification, thereby generating the third Person of the Trinity, but the disciples would have rejected this explanation. Jesus may not have said, "the Father will

25. Cited, Huston Smith, op. cit., p. 345.

26. Willard G. Oxtoby, op. cit., p. 232.

> give you another Counsellor, to be with you forever, even the Spirit of truth"; the assertion appears in the last of the Gospels to be written, in John, and is therefore disputed. But if the words were attributed to Jesus, it was because they reflected the disciples' understanding of their Pentecost experience. What they there witnessed, they were persuaded, was the dramatic arrival of a third party to the divine assembly, the Holy Spirit.[27]

The fact that its formulation even within Christianity possesses two versions again suggests an element in the doctrine recalcitrant to full understanding for "the Latin and Greek beliefs, as finally formulated, differed in conception. To the Latins God is one being in three persons or centres of consciousness; to the Greeks he is one being in three objects: as seen and thought he is three, as seeing and thinking he is one."[28] Nevertheless certain metaphors help to render the doctrine more accessible, even if one argues that "the disciples were brought to their understanding of God in three persons," in the sequence described earlier "once that understanding was in place, they projected it back to the beginning of time." For "if the divine 'triangle' has three 'sides' now it must always have had three sides."[29] In more general terms, "as water, ice, and steam, H_2O assumes states that are liquid, solid and gaseous while retaining its chemical identity, similarly, while God is fully one, God is also three."[30]

The use of water in this metaphor is helpful, for one obvious parallel in Hinduism to this triune conception of

27. Huston Smith, op. cit., p. 345.

28. J.G. Davies, op. cit., p. 73.

29. Huston Smith, op. cit., p. 345.

30. Ibid., p. 344.

God is the description of *Brahman* in Hinduism as *sat* (being) *cit* (consciousness) and *ānanda* (bliss). And this trinity is sometimes explained as follows:

> These three aspects, being, consciousness and bliss, are experienced as a unitary whole and not as separate attributes. They are inseparable in the same way that wetness, transparency and liquidity are inseparable properties of water.[31]

One might object however that the proper parallel with the doctrine of the trinity is not provided by the triune description of *Brahman* as *saccidānanda* but by the doctrine of the *trimūrti* in Hinduism, namely, by the view that Brahmā, Viṣṇu and Śiva represent three dimensions of one God. Even this example of *trimūrti* also promotes an understanding of the key concept of trinity that, according to Thomas Corbishley, "the godhead is a society of three divine persons, knowing and loving each other so entirely that not merely can none exist without the others, but in some mysterious way each is what the other is."[32] Kālidāsa's description of the Hindu trinity reminds one of this passage when he writes: "The one God appears as three — Brahmā, Viṣṇu, and Śiva. They are equals, none superior, none inferior. Sometimes, either Śiva or Viṣṇu is placed first; both yield place to Brahmā also."[33] It is worth noting though that Kālidāsa emphasizes their equality (although beginning with a recognition of their identity) while Thomas Corbishley emphasizes their identity.

---

31. David Godman, ed., *The Teachings of Sri Ramana Maharshi* (London and New York: Arkana, 1985), pp. 9-10.
32. Thomas Corbishley, cited by Huston Smith, op. cit., p. 346.
33. V. Sivaramakrishna, "The Mahasvami as a Guide to Poetic Appreciation", *Dilip* 30:4 (October–December 2004), p. 7.

4

Forms of Christianity

THE previous chapters covered the early development of Christianity and the events which culminated in the formulation of some of its central doctrines — to which most Christians in varying degrees offer their intellectual assent. That period however only covers the first four to five centuries of the history of Christianity, which over the centuries gradually spread to cover almost all of Europe, including Russia and, in more recent times, spread to other parts of the world such as the Americas, Africa and Asia. Even as it was spreading externally it was also evolving internally in ways which allow us to identify distinct branches within it, which recognize themselves as separate from each other although acknowledging a common membership of the worldwide Christian religious community. The three main branches usually identified in this context are those of (1) Roman Catholicism, (2) Protestantism, and (3) Eastern Orthodoxy. It is worth noting, however, that the Indonesian government treats Catholicism and Protestantism as two *distinct* religions and the same holds true for the government of China.

The discussion in which we have engaged so far basically possesses a Roman Catholic flavour, for Roman Catholicism was the original, and until the Eastern Church broke away from it in 1054, the only game in town, as it were. The split however may have had linguistic and cultural roots, represented by the use of Latin and Greek respectively in the liturgy. Some readers may be surprised by the fact that the language of liturgy might differ within Christianity, used as they might be to regarding Arabic as the liturgical language of Islam and Sanskrit as that of Hinduism. At the heart of Christianity lies the story of Jesus Christ, which can be told in any language, so Christianity does not possess its own sacred language as such, although a case might be made in favour of Latin in this regard. Christianity has been polyglot since its inception in this sense, inasmuch as the original language of the Old Testament is Hebrew and of the New Testament is Greek, while Jesus himself probably spoke some form of Aramaic. In this respect Christianity is more like Buddhism, whose basic canon, even in India was kept in different languages by different sects, one even using Sanskrit for this purpose, not to speak of the linguistic extensions it underwent when it moved beyond India into South-East Asia on the one hand and China, Korea and Japan on the other. Its message, like that of Christianity, could be delivered in any language without compromise.

To revert then to the main theme. The linguistic and cultural differences which characterized the Latin-speaking and Greek-speaking churches may have been the underlying factors but the overt basis of the split was a theological one, and the issue is encapsulated in a single Latin word *filioque*, which literally means "from the son." At issue was the question: Does the Holy Spirit "proceed" from the father, as the Greek Church believed, following the Nicene Creed, or from the father and son as the Latin Church now believed to be the case. The *filioque* clause, however, represented an issue not only of Trinitarian theology but also Church authority, as "Rome had added *filioque* to the creed without the action of a universal Church council. This pitted the Roman claim to be centre of authority against a Greek notion of Rome as one among five equally important patriarchies."[1] The break occurred in 1054.

The break between Roman Catholicism and Protestantism which occurred in the sixteenth century does not have a neat date attached to it but it was equally if not more consequential. It is associated with the name of Martin Luther (1483-1546). The issue, which ultimately snowballed into that of papal authority *versus* scriptural authority, arose out of protests over the sale of indulgences. The practice had evolved within the Church that people who visited relics on certain days and paid a certain amount of money had their stay in purgatory proportionately reduced. The fact that some of the funds thus gathered were to be used to build St Peter's Basilica in Rome added another convolution to the issue in the present context. In the debates which this challenge to the papal authority provoked, Luther moved increasingly away from the acceptance of Church as an interpreter of the Christian life to the text of the Bible itself. This text of the Bible, which was earlier not available to the laity, was now being translated into the various languages of Europe and becoming disseminated among the people with the introduction of printing. The issue evolved further in the direction not only of scriptural *versus*

1. Willard G. Oxtoby, op. cit., p. 246.

Church authority but also into the allied issue of whether one was saved by works or by faith. The Catholic Church's answer to the question had been that one was saved through both works and faith. But Martin Luther insisted that one was saved by faith alone.

> Taking up a key theme in Paul's New Testament letter to the Romans, Luther insists that humans are justified by faith alone. Both Paul and Luther take their stand on a confident experiential certainty. Luther refers to this as the inner guidance or testimony of the Holy Spirit. For Luther as for Paul, the dialectic is between faith and works. While the works Paul was downplaying were observance of Jewish commandments, the works that Luther downplays are the procedures of confession and penance in Latin Christianity. Paul's reaction was against the literal Torah, pitting against it the gospel or "good news" about Jesus, which was a preaching message in Paul's day but not yet a scriptural text. Now Luther, in contrast, makes scripture a key authority, indeed the fulcrum from which to exert leverage against the institutional Church.[2]

The clash between the Catholic Church and the Protestant movement produced a major convulsion in Christianity, which lasted for a few centuries, sometimes breaking out into open war. By the time the dust settled Italy and Spain remained firmly Roman Catholic but large parts of northern Europe has accepted Protestantism of one hue or another.

The basic features of these three main forms of Christianity: Roman Catholicism, Eastern Orthodoxy and Protestantism may now be examined, after this rapid survey of historical circumstances in which these transformations of the tradition came about.

---

2. Willard Oxtoby, op. cit., p. 280.

Roman Catholicism

Roman Catholicism regards itself as founded by St Peter, the direct disciple of Jesus himself, who, according to its understanding, was entrusted with his legacy in the following statement found in Matthew (16:18-19):

> I tell you, you are Peter, and on this rock I will build my Church. . . . I will give you the keys of the kingdom of Heaven, and whatever you bind on earth shall be bound in Heaven, and whatever you loose on earth shall be loosed in Heaven.

This is interpreted as Christ establishing an authority on earth who would continue to guide the community after his departure.

Such guidance may be interpreted in a twofold way: in terms of belief and in terms of practice. The twofold role of the Church as a teaching authority and as an agent administering sacraments thus came to the fore.[3]

The role of Church as a teaching authority, as it evolved in Roman Catholicism, amounted to this, that the scripture is to be understood in the light of the tradition of which the Church was a repository. Thus the Council of Trent (1546-63) declared that " . . . with the same devotion and reverence with which it accepts and venerates all the books of the Old and the New Testament, since one God is the author of both, it also accepts and venerates traditions concerned with faith and morals as having been received orally from Christ or inspired by the Holy Spirit and continuously preserved in the Catholic Church."[4] The underlying assumption is

---

3. Huston Smith, op. cit., pp. 347-48.

4. Cited in John Hick, *Philosophy of Religion* (4th edn.) (Englewood Cliffs, New Jersey: Prentice Hall, 1990), p. 57.

that direct and sole recourse to scripture may not be unproblemetical and that the authority of the Church might help resolve such difficulties. For instance: "Mark 10:11 tells us that 'whoever divorces his wife and marries another commits adultery.' Luke 16:18 concurs. But Matthew 5:32 enters a reservation: 'Except on the ground of unchastity.' What is the Christian to think?"[5]

A Christian might think many things but the integrity of Church depends on many Christians accepting the same thing to follow in situations such as these. It is easy to see how the Catholic Church would be led to the idea of papal infallibility, as to the process of argumentation there is no end. This doctrine, which can be easily misunderstood, maintains that when the "earthly head of the Church, [the] Pope, successor to St Peter in the bishopric of Rome" pronounces on matters of faith and morality (and on these alone), then he is protected form the possibility of error by the Holy Spirit.

The issue is a familiar one for Hindus under the word *śāstrārtha*. The word is routinely translated as a debate, specially a religious or theological debate, but its literal meaning is simply "[determining] the meaning of the scripture." It represents the Hindu way of resolving differences regarding the meaning of scripture. These differences are to be resolved through a debate between the disputing sides, with a neutral party acting as the umpire. The Catholic response to the problem is very different. It lay not in argument but consultation. It should be borne in mind that the Pope does not decide the matter

5. Huston Smith, op. cit., p. 348.

arbitrarily or whimsically but only "after studying a problem that relates to faith or morals as carefully as possible and with all available help from expert consultants."[6] In another way, however, the doctrine of papal infallibility displays a curious resemblance to what is considered to be the proper domain of Veda as a source of infallible knowledge according to Vedānta. It is well known that Vedānta accepts Vedas as authoritative only when they make pronouncements pertaining to *dharma* or *mokṣa*, just as papal utterances are considered infallible only when pertaining to matters of morals and faith.

The Church also administers the sacraments. This concept of sacraments finds a place in Hinduism in the form of *saṁskāras*, of which as many as forty are listed but which have long been standardized as sixteen. The most important of these are those of marriage (*vivāha*) and death (*antyeṣṭi*). From this perspective one might say that the Catholic Church believes in seven sacraments, just as classical Hinduism believes in sixteen. The comparison is helpful if one keeps it in mind that two Christian sacraments are not bound to the life cycle as we shall soon discover.

A list of seven sacraments is said to have become standard in Roman Catholicism by the twelfth century. These are: baptism, confirmation, holy matrimony, holy orders, sacrament of the sick (extreme unction), confession (or reconciliation) and mass (or Eucharist). Baptism is performed on the infant with holy water and the child gets its name at this time. At confirmation the grown-up child accepts the responsibilities of the membership of the Church.

6. Huston Smith, op. cit., p. 349.

Then follows marriage for those who choose to marry (holy matrimony) or ordination for those who want to become monks (holy orders). Finally, as the curtain falls on life, one is commended to God in the sacrament of the sick. These sacraments are like sacred punctuations in the sentence of our life as it gets written out. They are tied to biological events or decisions. The life of the Hindu has more punctuation marks but some parallels are obvious. Baptism contains an element of *nāmakaraṇa* while *upanayana* can be seen as an elaborate confirmation. The Christian juxtaposition of holy matrimony and holy orders is interesting, as Hinduism is more prone to emphasize the radical disjunction of the two. Similarly, the Hindu *antyeṣṭi* prepares the soul for the final journey after the person's death while the Christian sacrament (more thoughtfully?) starts preparing one for that final journey while one is still alive.

It should not be difficult for a Hindu to grasp the sentiment associated with these sacraments. Perhaps no human being will have difficulty relating to them as they correspond broadly to the rites of passage all of us undergo. It is now time to turn to the other two sacraments we had reserved for later discussion.

The first of these is confession or reconciliation. It is based on the belief that "if one confesses one's sin to God in the presence of one of God's delegates, a priest, and truly repents of the sin committed and honestly resolves (whether or not this resolve proves effective) to avoid it in the future, one will be forgiven."[7] The priest of course is totally

7. Huston Smith, op. cit., p. 350.

forbidden from revealing the confession to anyone.

The practice of confession has parallels in the Indic religious tradition. The form in which we find it in Buddhism is not identical with the Christian but can be related to it. The fortnightly meeting of the monks, called *uposatha* in Pāli, contained an element of confession. After the *pātimokkha* or the rules of the Order had been recited at such an assembly "every monk was asked whether he had committed any breach of the rules in the preceding fortnight. If the offence was of a light nature, absolution was given on his confessing it in public."[8] The contrast, however, with the Christian confession is obvious, wherein it is moral and spiritual in nature rather than part of a formal structure of discipline. Moreover, Buddhism is a non-theistic tradition and the heart of the Christian confession lies in its being made to God. An important similarity though should not go unnoticed: that both the traditions clearly specify the method and manner in which the confession is to be made — it is not a merely personal affair. And as it is not a purely personal affair, both the Christian and Buddhist descriptions of it are quite explicit in defining the valid party in front of whom the confession, once made, is acceptable.

This idea of the right party before whom a confession may be made was also an element in Mahatma Gandhi's experiments with truth. One such incident relates to the confession he made to his father early in life, after he began smoking on the sly and stealing for the purpose. He however could not bear the idea of deceiving his parents.

8. R.C. Majumdar, ed., *The Age of Imperial Unity* (Bombay: Bharatiya Vidya Bhavan, 1968), p. 375.

I decided at last to write out the confession, to submit it to my father, and ask his forgiveness. I wrote it on a slip of paper and handed it to him myself. In this note not only did I confess my guilt, but I asked adequate punishment for it, and closed with a request to him not to punish himself for my offence. I also pledged myself never to steal in future.

I was trembling as I handed the confession to my father. He was then suffering from a fistula and was confined to bed. His bed was a plain wooden plank. I handed him the note and sat opposite the plank.

He read it through, and pearl-drops trickled down his cheeks, wetting the paper. For a moment he closed his eyes in thought and then tore up the note. He had sat up to read it. He again lay down. I also cried. I could see my father's agony. If I were a painter I could draw a picture of the whole scene today. It is still so vivid in my mind.

Those pearl-drops of love cleansed my heart, and washed my sin away. Only he who has experienced such love can know what it is. As the hymn says:

> Only he
> Who is smitten with the arrows of love,
> Knows its power.

This was, for me, an object-lesson in *ahiṁsā*. Then I could read in it nothing more than a father's love, but today I know that it was pure *ahiṁsā*. When such *ahiṁsā* becomes all-embracing, it transforms everything it touches. There is no limit to its power.

This sort of sublime forgiveness was not natural to my father. I had thought that he would be angry, say hard things, and strike his forehead. But he was so wonderfully peaceful, and I believe this was due to my clean confession. A clean confession, combined with a promise never to commit the sin again, when offered before one who has the right to receive it, is the purest type of repentance. I know that my

> confession made my father feel absolutely safe about me, and increased his affection for me beyond measure.[9]

The *Manusmṛti* (XI:228-29) also accepts confession as a form of penance but does not institutionalize it the way Roman Catholicism does. Given the fact of Hinduism's priestly orientation, which it shares with the Catholic Church, it is interesting that Hindu priests were not formally involved in it. Perhaps the individualism of the Hindu tradition proved too much for it, whereby even families often did not have their meal together, with each member eating at his or her convenience.

The most significant Christian sacrament has, however, been saved for discussion at the very end. It is known by several names: the Eucharist, the Mass, Holy Communion or the Lord's Supper. The Eucharist is from the Greek wherein it means gratitude. From this point of view it is a rite of thanks-giving. The Mass is from Latin *missa*, "a form of the verb 'to send.' The ancient liturgy contained two dismissals, one for people interested in Christianity but not yet baptized, which preceded the sacrament of the Eucharist, and a second for fully initiated Christians after it had been celebrated. Coming as it did between the two dismissals, the rite first came to be called *missa* and then, by transliteration, the Mass."[10] It is called Holy Communion because it is a way of communing with God, and the name, the Lord's Supper for the rite has its origin in what Jesus

---

9. *Gandhi's Autobiography: The Story of My Experiments with Truth* by M.K. Gandhi, tr. Mahadev Desai (Washington, D.C.: Public Affairs Press, 1940), pp. 41-42.

10. Huston Smith, op. cit., p. 350.

Christ said and did at the last supper he had with his followers before he was crucified. The following description constitutes a representative account of those events:

> The central feature of the Mass is the re-enactment of Christ's Last Supper in which, as he gave his disciples bread and wine, he said, "This is my blood that is shed for you." It is false to the Catholic concept of this Sacrament to think of it as a commemoration through which priest and communicants elevate their spirits by symbolic remembrance of Christ's example. The Mass provides an actual transfusion of spiritual energy from God to human souls. In a general way this holds for all the Sacraments, but for the Mass it holds uniquely. For the Catholic Church teaches that in the host and the chalice, the consecrated bread and wine, Christ's human body and blood are actually present. They consider his words, "This is my body. . . . This is my blood," explicit on this point. When a priest utters these words of consecration, therefore, the change that they effect in the elements is not one of significance only. The elements may not appear different afterward; analysis would register no chemical change. In technical language this means that their "accidents" remain as they were, but their "substance" is transubstantiated. We might say the Eucharist conveys God's grace as a boat conveys its passengers, whereas the other sacraments convey grace as a letter conveys meaning. For the letter to have meaning, intelligence is required in addition to the paper and ink marks; so too in Sacraments other than the Eucharist, God's power is necessary in addition to the instruments of the sacrament. But in the Mass spiritual nourishment is literally to be had from the elements themselves. It is exactly as important for the Christians' spiritual life to feast upon them as it is for their bodily lives to partake of food. Opening your mouth for the Bread of Life, writes Saint Francis de Sales,
>
> > *Full of faith, hope and charity, receive Him, in whom, by whom, and for whom, you believe, hope and love. . . .*

> *Represent to yourself that as the bee, after gathering from the flowers the dew of heaven and the choicest juice of the earth, reduces them into honey and carries it into her hive, so the priest, having taken from the altar the Savior of the world, the true Son of God, who, as the dew, is descended from heaven, and the true Son of the Virgin, who, as a flower is sprung from the earth of our humanity, puts him as delicious food into your mouth and into your body.*

> This personal presence of God in the elements of the Mass distinguishes it significantly from the other Sacraments, but it does not vitiate the common bond that united them all. Each is a means by which God, through Christ's mystical body, literally infuses into human souls the supernatural power that enables them so to live in this world that in the world to come they may have life everlasting.[11]

A Hindu who attends the Mass the first time is likely to return from it in a state of mild shock, because it turns normal Hindu notions of morality on their head. Hindus may drink alcohol, but they are told by their culture not to drink. Hindus may eat meat, but they are told by their culture to be vegetarians if they could. For a person with such a background the potential alcoholism of wine being drunk and that too as blood, and the potential cannibalism of bread being made into a (human) body to be eaten is appalling. Christianity for a moment appears to be a degenerate *tāntrika* sect. And nothing more, as this is its central ritual. Moreover, the idea that by drinking blood and eating flesh one communicates with some divinity sounds primitive in the extreme.

---

11. Huston Smith, op. cit., pp. 350-51.

The first step towards relating to this sacrament in the right spirit is to view it as a Christian. Just as an onlooker who thinks a Hindu is worshipping a phallus when he bows to the *Śiva-liṅga* misses the point, so does the Hindu miss the point if he or she considers the Mass as an alcoholic and cannibalistic orgy.

Perhaps the proper view is to look upon it as a *śrāddha* periodically performed for Jesus Christ according to his own instructions, at which he is actually present.

Eastern Orthodoxy

One should begin by noting the ways in which Roman Catholicism and Eastern Orthodoxy are similar rather than apart. They both accept the dual role of the Church as teaching authority and sacramental agent, and, as sacramental agent accept the seven sacraments just discussed above. Although there is no difference in the administration of the sacraments as such, there is a difference in how the role of the clergy is viewed in relation to the laity. The Roman Catholic Church emphasizes the distinctness of the office of the clergy by virtue of its papal structure and insistence on celibacy on part of the clergy. But in Eastern Orthodoxy, though the clergy is distinct from the laity, it is less separate. Laity has more say in the selection of bishops on the one hand, and, on the other, priests need not be celibate in Eastern Orthodoxy. More difference surfaces in their understanding of the role of the Church as a teaching authority. The basic conviction about the need for role of the Church as teaching authority is shared: "Left to private interpretation the Christian faith would degenerate into conflicting claims and a mass of uncertainties. It is the Church's responsibility to insure against this, and God enables it to do so; the Holy Spirit preserves its official statements from error."[12] Difference arises when it comes to the extent to which such action by the Church is required and the manner in which it should act. As to the extent, Eastern Orthodoxy believes that the exercise of authority in this domain should be restricted to matters mentioned in the scripture. Thus "in principle only issues that are mentioned in the scripture can qualify, which is to say that the Church can interpret doctrines but it cannot initiate them. In practice the Church has exercised her prerogative as interpreter only seven times, in the Seven Ecumenical Councils, all of which were held before 787."[13] The point has to be addressed carefully. Certain beliefs and practices may be part of the Church; the issue is whether they call for dogmatic pronouncement the way the Catholic Church has made it in the case of the Immaculate Conception, or the bodily assumption of Mary. It is worth noting that the last was "introduced in practice but without proclaiming it as dogma"[14] in Eastern Orthodoxy. Thus what are considered as "developments in doctrine" by one party are considered as "innovations" by the other.

Some scholars have argued that the difference in the temper of these two branches of Christianity may lie in the fact that academic institutionalization characterizes the experience of Western Christianity more than the Eastern. "When we reach for an image to epitomize Roman

12. Huston Smith, op. cit., p. 352.
13. Ibid.
14. Ibid., p. 353.

Catholicism, we think of the Middle Ages. Its counterpart in Eastern Orthodoxy is the Church Fathers."[15]

Not only is the number of items on which the teaching authority of the Church may be exercised less in the case of Eastern Orthodoxy, the manner in which it might be exercised is also different in Eastern Orthodoxy. It will be recalled that one of the issues underlying the split between Roman Catholicism and Eastern orthodoxy was that of authority. The Greek notion of Rome was of a partner, while the Roman notion of Constantinople was of it being under Rome. It should not come as a surprise then that not only does Eastern Orthodoxy not acknowledge the Pope of Roman Catholicism, it has no Pope of its own either but rather four Patriarchies, although the Patriarch of Constantinople is the titular head. This difference in structure goes hand in hand with a slightly different interpretation of the "conscience of the Church," whose consensus in the Roman Catholic case is ultimately reflected in the papal pronouncement. In the Eastern Orthodox conception it is the ecclesiastical councils which serve to provide a focus to the diffused consensus of all Christians. So in the Eastern Orthodox conception, it is the Christians in general who are prevented by the Holy Spirit from lapsing into error rather than through the Pope.

Apart from these distinctions in the role of the Church as a teaching authority, observers like to point out that Eastern Orthodox Christianity "has most emphasized the corporate nature of the Church, both the ecclesiastical equality of its members (as against Catholicism), and their

15. Huston Smith, op. cit., p. 353.

solidarity (as against Protestantism)."[16] While all Christians accept the view that they are "members of one another," Eastern Orthodoxy puts this additional spin on it that "one can be damned alone, but saved only with others."[17]

This recognition of the corporate character imparts to Eastern Orthodoxy a *tāntrika* character. Unfortunately the way the word *tantra* entered the English language has made it a byword for sex. What one has in mind here is the fact that the literature of Tantra downplays the distinctions in Smārta Hinduism between the twice-borns and the rest, in a way reminiscent of Eastern Orthodoxy's more liberal approach to the laity. But another point is of even greater significance. Tantra emphasizes the deification of the spiritual aspirant — one is exhorted to worship a God by becoming like one. This finds a parallel of sorts in the Eastern Orthodox view that the "aim of every life should be union with God — actual deification, by grace, to the point of sharing the divine life; *theosis* is the Greek word for the doctrine that this sharing is possible."[18]

Protestantism

Protestant Christianity is in some ways easier to present by comparison with other forms of Christianity, and in other ways harder. To take up the hard part first: the break between Roman Catholicism and Protestantism came in the form of small doses rather than one big event, unlike the case of Eastern Orthodoxy. Moreover, the Protestant

---

16. Huston Smith, op. cit., p. 355.
17. Ibid., p. 354.
18. Ibid., p. 356.

movement gives at least the appearance of being extremely fragmented, for it follows "four main courses — Baptist, Lutheran, Calvinists, and Anglican"[19] and these themselves subdivide into over nine-hundred denominations in the USA alone![20] And as for the range of religious conceptions these represent, for most Protestants Jesus Christ is the son of God, but for a denomination known as Unitarian-Universalist he is a son of God in the same sense as you are a son of God! So if, as a Hindu, you get caught in a situation where you must identify yourself in terms of a Christian denomination, you now know which one to choose.

We shall cut across the Gordian knots of Protestantism's complex history and bewildering variety with two strokes of the Alexandrian sword. We shall bypass the history of its break-up with the Roman Catholic Church with the help of the following comments of Huston Smith:

> The causes that led to the break between Roman Catholicism and what came to be known as Protestant Christianity are complex and still in dispute. Political economy, nationalism, Renaissance individualism, and a rising concern over ecclesiastical abuses all played their part. They do not, however, camouflage the fact that the basic cause was religious, a difference in Christian perspective between Roman Catholicism and Protestantism. As we are concerned here with ideas rather than history, we shall say no more about the causes of the Protestant Reformation. Instead, we shall be content to treat the sixteenth century — Luther, Calvin, the Ninety-five Theses, the Diet of Worms, King Henry VIII, the Peace of Augsburg — as a vast tunnel. The Western Church entered that tunnel whole; it emerged from

19. Huston Smith, op. cit., p. 347.

20. Ibid., p. 347.

> it in two sections. More accurately, it emerged in several sections, for Protestantism is not so much a Church as a movement of Churches.[21]

And for its teeming denominational variety we shall recognize that "actually, 85 per cent of all Protestants belong to twelve denominations"[22] reminiscent of Jesus' choice of twelve apostles, or even the twelve tribes of Israel if one delves deeper in history,[23] so that "considering the freedom of belief Protestantism affirms in principle, the wonder lies not in its diversity but in the extent to which Protestants have managed to stay together."[24] Moreover, "Protestant divisions reflect differing national origins in Europe or differing social groupings in the United States more than they do differing theologies"[25] One might say that Protestantism is as profligate with its sects as classical Hinduism was with its castes.

This point regarding the national origins may specially interest the Hindus as the Anglican Church is the official Church of England, which was also the established Church of British India until formally disestablished in the 1920s. So India has been subject not just to British but Anglican rule as well. But the Anglican Church is of special interest from another point of view. This form of Protestantism is very close to Roman Catholicism, but for the fact that it rejects papal authority — a step King Henry VIIIth, the Tudor monarch, had to undertake so that he could beget an heir

21. Huston Smith, op. cit., p. 357.
22. Ibid., p. 361.
23. J.G. Davies, op. cit., p. 52.
24. Huston Smith, op. cit., p. 361.
25. Ibid., p. 362.

to the throne. Professor Wilfred Cantwell Smith therefore used to remark that because he considers himself an Anglican, he can claim to be both a Roman Catholic and a Protestant at the same time, and because he considers himself a Hindu, he can claim to be both a Christian and a Muslim at the same time!

To turn now to the teachings of Protestantism. So far as its views on the Church as a sacramental authority is concerned, it admits of only two sacraments: Baptism and Eucharist. And so far as the Church as a teaching authority is concerned, it allows each individual to shape his or her faith with direct encounter with the Bible, thereby eliminating the intermediation of the Church. This follows from Luther's Pronouncement that "everyone must do his own believing as he will have to do his own dying."[26]

These few words conceal a world of difference between the concepts of revelation in the Roman Catholicism (and Eastern Orthodoxy) and Protestantism. The concept of revelation in Roman Catholicism may be said to be propositional.

> According to this view, the content of revelation is a body of truths expressed in statements or propositions. Revelation is the imparting to people of divinely authenticated truths. In the words of the older *Catholic Encyclopedia*, "Revelation may be defined as the communication of some truth by God to a rational creature through means which are beyond the ordinary course of nature."[27]

---

26. Cited, Huston Smith, op. cit., p. 357.
27. John H. Hick, op. cit., p. 56.

The concept of revelation undergoes a sea-change in Protestantism and is often referred to as the non-propositional view of revelation (technically known as the *heilsgeschichtliche* view). "According to this non-propositional view, the content of revelation is not a body of truths about God, but God coming within the orbit of human experience by acting in history."[28] It is also worth noting that "this non-propositional conception of revelation is connected with the modern renewed emphasis upon the personal character of God and the thought that the divine-human personal relationship consists of something more than the promulgation and reception of theological truths."[29]

The three expressions which are often said to summarize the Protestant doctrines are now easier to grasp. These are (1) *sola dei* (God alone); (2) *sola scriptura* (scripture alone) and (3) *sola fidé* (faith alone).

SOLA DEI

The very word Protestant helps to grasp this point, for the word protestant literally means to testify for (just as the word prophet means pro-phet or to speak for). For this raises the question: To speak for whom, on whose behalf? The answer is: God.

The point is twofold. First of all, the focus of Catholicism had shifted from God to all kinds of other things — to the saints, to the rituals and so on. Protestantism claimed to bring the focus back to where it belonged, namely, God.

28. John H. Hick, op. cit., p. 64.

29. Ibid., p. 56.

The second level of significance is existential rather than historical: We constantly tend to lose our focus on God and need to refocus on him all the time. This turning our attention away from God, and the tendency to accord to things other than God the status of God is what the Protestant principle warns us against: "Stated philosophically, it warns against absolutizing the relative. Stated theologically, it warns against idolatry."[30] Huston Smith proceeds to explain that these are

> very hard truths to keep in mind; so hard that people continually let them slip and proceed to equate God with something they can see or touch or at least conceptualize more precisely than the infinite. Early on they equated God with statues, until prophets — the first "protestants" or protesters on this score — rose up to denounce their transpositions, dubbing their pitiful substitutes idols, or "little pieces of form." Later, people stopped deifying wood and stone, but this did not mean that idolatry ended. While the secular world proceeded to absolutize the state, or the self, or human intellect, Christians fell to absolutizing dogmas, the Sacraments, the Church, the Bible, or personal religious experience. To think that Protestantism devalues these or doubts that God is involved in them is to misjudge it seriously. It does, however, insist that none of them is God.[31]

The theological difficulties which beset this ideal are highlighted by John Hick as follows:

> The difficulty involved in maintaining such a faith in practice, even within a culture that has been permeated for centuries by monotheistic teaching, is evidenced by the

30. Huston Smith, op. cit., p. 359.

31. Ibid.

> polytheistic and henotheistic elements in our own life. A religiously sensitive visitor from another planet would doubtless report that we divide our energies in the service of many deities — the god of money, of a business corporation, of success, and of power, the status gods, and (for a brief period once a week) the God of Judaic-Christian faith. When we rise above this practical polytheism, it is generally into the henotheistic devotion to the nation, or to the American way of life, in order to enjoy our solidarity with an in-group against the out-groups.[32]

SOLA SCRIPTURA

It is the scriptures which contain an account of God moving within the orbit of human experience in the form of Jesus Christ. So one must, first of all, turn to this account and encounter it oneself (rather than through the Church). Once this happens one discovers an epistemological option, namely, that events could be interpreted in an ordinary secular way, or as representing God's action in history.

> The same epistemological pattern — the interpreting in a distinctive way of events that are in themselves capable of being construed either naturalistically or religiously — runs through the New Testament. Here again, in the story of a man, Jesus of Nazarath, and a movement which arose in connection with him, there are ambiguous data. It is possible to see him simply as a self-appointed prophet who got mixed up in politics, clashed with the Jerusalem priesthood, and had to be eliminated. It is also possible, with the New Testament writers, to see him as the Messiah of God giving himself to the renewing of humankind.[33]

So which of the two interpretations is one going to choose?

---

32. John H. Hick, op. cit., p. 7.

33. Ibid. p. 67.

SOLA FIDÉ

The decision has to be a leap of faith, for the evidence is so exquisitely uncertain that truth could go either way. This is one way of understanding the Protestant emphasis on faith. The other has to do with Luther's own experience. Luther was a very conscientious priest but found that no matter how hard he tried he could not measure up to the ideal.

> He wrestled with his own sense of unworthiness and inability to find relief through the monastic practices. But a momentous experience changed his life: his so-called tower experience. Preparing for lectures on the *Psalms*, he was bothered by the references to God's righteousness. Turning to *Romans* 3:21-24, he read:
>
>> *Now God's righteousness is revealed apart from the law, testified to by the Law and the Prophets, God's righteousness which is through faith in Jesus Christ unto all who believe. For there is no difference; all have sinned and fall short of the glory of God, being justified as a gift by his grace through the redemption that is in Christ Jesus.*
>
> Raging at God over the impossibility of living up to the righteousness of God, Luther suddenly saw a totally different meaning: The righteousness of God is a *forgiving* righteousness, by which God makes us righteous through Christ. This theology of "justification through faith by grace" henceforth became the heart of Luther's theology, leading him ultimately to reject all ideas of justification through one's own monastic practices or through the works of the church: penance, the sacraments, absolution, and the like.[34]

The belief also produced the startling conclusion: that monasticism could also be dispensed with if salvation came from faith alone.

---

34. Theodore M. Ludwig, *The Sacred Paths* (Upper Saddle Rive, New Jersey: Prentice Hall, 2001), p. 395.

> By the mid-1520s the forces Luther had unleashed were pulling in diverse directions. Different people expected different types of reform. On one agenda, the life of a priestly or monastic vocation, he set a personal example. His teachings spurred a dozen nuns to leave the convent in Wittenberg, three of whom went back to their families but the other nine of whom were now homeless. Luther as a matchmaker found husbands for eight, and then took the last, Katherina von Bora, as his own wife. We do not have the details, but surmise that moral concern, even ideological conviction, played a greater initial role than romance. In the course of time they had six children and also adopted four orphans. In his writing *Concerning Married Life*, Luther suggests that even washing diapers is an act that can be ennobled by faith. And he set a pattern for married clergy in Protestantism that, whatever else may be said for it, has at least pressed clergy to counsel the married people among their flocks on the basis of practical experience as well as theory.[35]

These discussions of Christian doctrines might appear very remote to the Hindu, unless one realizes that a similar issue also arose within medieval Vaiṣṇavism, specially in Tamil Nadu. Rāmānuja (*c.* 1017–1137) had established the philosophical school of Viśiṣṭādvaita Vedānta and thereby laid the philosophical foundations of Śrīvaiṣṇavism. The system of Rāmānuja emphasized devotion and grace as means to salvation. The Śrīvaiṣṇava tradition, however, later forked into the two branches of Vaṭakaḷai (or the Northern School) and Teṅgaḷai (or the Southern School). One of the points on which they differed reincarnates the works *versus* faith controversy within Christianity. The issue in the case

35. Willard Oxtoby, op. cit., p. 282.

of Śrīvaiṣṇavism was the following: Must a human being do something to secure God's grace or is that grace totally independent of human volition. The Northern School felt that while grace comes from God, some human effort may also be required to attain it on the analogy of the mother monkey who carries her young from tree to tree but the child needs to cling to her. The Southern School, by contrast, chose to rely solely on God's grace, just as a cat carries its young in its mouth, with the young not having to do anything at all. The two arguments were code named monkey logic and cat logic. The argument continues. Perhaps a wrinkle can be provided by the marsupials in Australia, where the young of the kangaroo just sits in the pouch of the mother as illustrating a third way of how God's grace might operate.

5

Christian Scriptures

THE reader is doubtless already aware of the fact that the fundamental and foundational scripture of Christianity is the Bible, a word which literally means a book and here the book.

This book, as it exists, is of considerable size and consists of two distinct parts known as the Old Testament and the New Testament. The covenant which God had made with the Jews was now replaced by the covenant he had made with them through Jesus Christ, so the history of the Jews and God's dealing with them, which constitutes the account of God's covenant with the Jews, came to be looked upon as the Old Testament.

Let us discuss this so-called Old Testament first. The first point to note here then is the the "Old Testament is the Jewish *Tanakh,* which makes the Christian Bible unique among the world's scriptures by including the canon of a different religion."[1]

The Jews call their own scripture *Tanakh,* for obviously it has not been superseded from their point of view. Scholars prefer to refer to the Old Testament as the Hebrew Bible or

1. James Fieser and John Powers, *Scriptures of the West* (2nd edn.) (New York: McGraw Hill, 2004), p. 98.

the Tanakh, when speaking of it in a general way out of respect of this fact.

This word *Tanakh* is an acronym, which gained currency in the Middle Ages, and is constituted by the initial words of the three divisions which characterize the Hebrew Bible:

> Torah: which refers to the first five books of the Bible: Genesis, Exodus, Leviticus, Numbers and Deuteronomy.
>
> Neviim: consisting of the category of (a) the Former Prophets: Joshua, Judges, Samuel, Kings and (b) Latter Prophets: Isaiah, Jeremiah, Ezekeil, the Twelve (Hosea, Joel, Amos, Obadiah, Jonah, Micah, Nahum, Habakkuk, Zephaniah, Haggai, Zechariah, Malachi).
>
> Ketuvim: which consists of Psalms, Job, Proverbs, Ruth, Song of Songs, Ecclesiates, Lamentations, Esther, Daniel, Ezra-Nehemiah, Chronicles.

The word Torah literally means "teaching," the word Neviim literally means "Prophets" and the word Ketuvim literally means "writings." These divisions were already in place by 90 BCE, when they received the official stamp of the Sanhedrin or Jewish Council in the city of Jabneh in Palestine.[2]

For the reader who must have now begun to wonder by now what is all this about, it might be helpful to note that

> The theme of the Old Testament is that of God's dealings with Israel from the time when the twelve tribes were united under Moses to form a nation. This story is set within a universal context by the opening chapters of Genesis which recount God's creation of heaven and earth and of man "in

2. James Fieser and John Powers, op. cit., pp. 32-33.

his own image" (*Genesis*, 27). Man, however, dissatisfied with his position of subjection to God within the created order, rebelled against his Maker, and soon "all flesh had corrupted his way upon the earth" (*Genesis* vi, 12). God's method of dealing with this situation was to choose one man, Abraham, out of all the fallen mass of mankind, whose descendants were to form a nucleus of faithful people, and to be both the recipients of the divine blessing and the source of its mediation to all men.

It was these descendants who were delivered by God from bondage in Egypt, united to him in a Covenant, led into the promised land and provided with a King as the divine representative — a King who was at the same time the Messiah, which means the (Lord's) Anointed. Despite the warnings of the prophets, the Israelites did not persevere in the way of righteousness and so they were brought to the suffering of the Exile in Babylonia. Then, in penitence, hope revived and they looked forward to a restoration when the powers of evil should be overthrown, when God's Kingdom or rule should be set up, exercised either directly or through his promised Messiah, and a New Covenant should be established (*Jeremiah* XXXI, 31). Neither the events immediately succeeding the return from Babylon nor the short-lived independence of the Jews under the Maccabean house satisfied this hope, as successive foreign powers held them in submission, from the Persians in the sixth century BCE to the Romans in the latter half of the first. But the hope did not die, and when St Luke, in the second chapter of his Gospel, referred to Simeon as a man "looking for the consolation of Israel" he was describing an attitude typical of the majority of the Jews of his day. The New Testament affirmation — and it is this that constituted it in the understanding of its first proclaimers as the Gospel or Good News — is to the effect that this hope was now in process of fulfilment through the mission of Jesus of Nazareth.[3]

The Torah covers the account up to the point of entry of the people in the Promised Land.

The record of the history of God's dealing with "his people" from that point onwards until the coming of Jesus is covered in the Neviim and the Ketuviim. This is how the Hebrew Bible brings us to the brink of the New Testament. The key point to bear in mind is that, as a result of persistent historical setbacks, the Jews were looking forward "to a Davidic king, a prophet like Moses, or a perfect priest, although the actual term *messiah* was rarely used"[4] around the time.

The arrival of Jesus on the scene put history in fast-forward, and, briefly put, those who began to think and continued to think that Jesus answered to the description of the Messiah and even came to look upon him as the Son of God became Christians, and those who did not accept him as the Messiah continued to be Jews.

It is among the Christians that the second part of the Bible, the New Testament, evolved and took shape. "By the fourth century BCE, the term New Testament was commonly used to refer to a collection of 27 early Christian texts composed in Greek." The language of the Tanakh by contrast was Hebrew.

---

3. J.G. Davies, "Christianity: The Early Church", in R.C. Zaehner, ed., *The Concise Encyclopedia of Living Faiths* (Boston: Beacon Press, 1967), p. 51. Parts of this passage have been cited earlier.

4. James Fieser and John Powers, op. cit., p. 95.

Just as the texts of the Old Testament were classified into three categories, the texts of the New Testament are classified into five categories as follows:

Gospels: Matthew, Mark, Luke, John

Book of Acts

Letters of Paul: Romans, 1 and 2 Corinthians, Galatians, Ephesians, Philippians, Colossians, 1 and 2 Thessalonians, 1 and 2 Timothy, Titus, Philemon, Hebrews

General Letters: Letter of James; 1 and 2 Letters of Peter; 1, 2 and 3 Letters of John; Letter of Jude

Book of Revelation

Just as historical logic underlay the "Old Testament," historical logic also underlies the New Testament. The Gospels contain the account of the life of Jesus. "Mark, Matthew, and Luke are referred to as *synoptic gospels,* since they give very similar account of Jesus' life and teachings."[5] The gospel of John, which was even "initially considered heretical by some Church fathers, . . . presents an account that is 90 per cent different in content."[6] The next textual category, the Book of Acts "discusses the spread of early Christianity immediately after Jesus. Of particular concern is the relationship of Christianity to Judaism in view of the large number of non-Jewish converts." In the same spirit, "more than half of Acts chronicles the conversion and missionary journeys of Paul."[7] To the next category belong the letters of Paul, which "contain encouragement and

5. James Fieser and John Powers, op. cit., pp. 99-100.

6. Ibid., p. 100.

7. Ibid.

instructions to the churches he helped establish."[8] Similarly, the next textual category, that of General Letters, consists of "tracts or sermons addressing problems in early Church communities."[9] The last and final category, the Book of Revelation, "describes a series of apocalyptic visions which contain instructions to Christians to remain faithful in the face of Roman persecution."[10]

At this point history outstrips scripture because Constantine becomes emperor and in CE 313 proclaimed tolerance of Christianity. He then sponsored a meeting of the bishops at Nicea in 325, where the New Testament is accorded the status of authoritative Christian scripture.

---

8. James Fieser and John Powers, op. cit., p. 100.
9. Ibid.
10. Ibid.

6

Christianity in India

The Arrival of Christianity in India

There is a persistent legend, although discounted by most scholars, that Christianity was brought to India by St Thomas. The first clear allusion to this is found in the *Acts of Thomas* assigned to the third century. Stephen Neill summarizes its evidence as follows:

> Here we read that, in the division of the world among the apostles, India fell to the lot of Thomas. This apostle, however, declared that he, a man of Israel, could not go to preach the gospel among Indians whose language he did not know. The Lord then arranged for Thomas, who was a skilled carpenter, to be sold as a slave to one Abbanes, an agent of Gundaphorus, king of India, who was in Jerusalem looking for skilled craftsmen. Much is told of the adventures of Thomas in India, and of course of the miraculous conversion of the king. Scholars had tended to treat all this as mere romance; but the discovery in north-west India of coins of a certain King Gundobar, who must have reigned in the second half of the first century CE, suggested that at least some facts must lie behind the romance. Clearly there was some connection between Persia and India over the passes, and the writer of the *Acts* may well have had some knowledge of the presence of Christians in India at that early date. But these Christians must have lived in what is now the Punjab, nowhere near the Kerala of the Church of

the Thomas Christians.[1]

Further evidence of Christian presence in India is provided by the text called *Christian Topography* by Cosmas Indicopleustes "who actually made the journey to India, as his name implies, between CE 525 and 530."[2] He writes:

> . . . in the island of Taprobane (Ceylon) . . . there is a church with clergy and a congregation of Christians . . . and such is also the case in the land called Male where the pepper grows. . . . The island hath also a church of Persian Christians who have settled there, and a presbyter who is appointed from Persia, and all the apparatus of public worship. But the natives and their kings are heathen.[3]

The account clearly refers to the presence of a Christian Church in Sri Lanka and south India, but one of Persian rather than indigenous Christians, although it is possible that it might have gained some local followers. The form of Christianity primarily known in Persia was the Nestorian — according to which Jesus possessed two separate persons — one human and the other divine. This doctrine was considered heretical from the point of view of the orthodox Church but was popular in parts of Asia for a while.

Christian presence in India is placed on firmer ground by the identification of five copper plates whose dating is controversial but which are usually assigned to *c.* CE 800.

> These plates are written in the old Tamil script, but the signatures of witnesses include a number in Pahlavi (middle

---

1. Stephen Neill, *The Story of the Christian Church in India and Pakistan* (Grand Rapids, Michigan: William B. Eerdmans Publishing Company, 1970), p. 17.
2. Stephen Neill, op. cit., p. 17.
3. Cited, ibid., p. 18.

> Persian), Arabic in Kufic characters, and a kind of Persian in Hebrew characters. The king assigns to the church in Quilon a number of slaves, and at the same time commits to the Christians the administration of customs, the care of weights and measures, and probably custody of the official seal. Once again we notice the presence of strangers and foreigners. But we see something of the process by which an alien community became deeply rooted in Indian soil, and came to feel itself to be part of the Indian people. Doubtless the slaves of the "Company" were baptized. The traders who settled down permanently, having come without their wives, married Indian women, and thus the original Persian element diminished as the percentage of Indian blood increased.[4]

There is some dispute whether this body of Christians should be regarded as "Indian Christians"[5] or a group of Persian merchants.[6] Despite its location in India "it retained its sense of foreignness, and emphasized it at two points. For centuries the bishop came from the original homeland of the Church; as far as we know, no one born in India was consecrated to the Episcopate until the seventeenth century. And the divine service was always conducted in Syriac and never in the language of south India,"[7] so that even to this day it is known as the Syrian Church.

Christianity in the Medieval Period

The rise of Islam meant that the Church of South India was cut off from the Christian world and when "Islam

---

4. Stephen Neill, op. cit., pp. 18-19.
5. A.L. Basham, op. cit., p. 343.
6. Stephen Neill, op. cit., pp. 18-19.
7. Ibid., p. 19.

stamped out both Zoroastrianism and Christianity in Persia, the Indian Christians turned for guidance to the Patriarch of Antioch, and [have] maintained contact with Syria to this day."[8] A.L. Basham describes the later history of the Church as follows:

> When European travellers again visited India they noticed the Christian churches of the South. Marco Polo, at the end of the 13th century, saw the tomb of St Thomas, and remarked on its popularity as a place of pilgrimage. But the Syrian church was corrupt. There is no evidence that Indian Christians ever accepted the doctrine of transmigration, but many Hindu customs had been adopted, and the Malabar Christians, like the Buddhists and Jainas before them, were in the process of becoming a rather heterodox Hindu sect. Jesuit missionaries of the 16th and 17th centuries succeeded in preventing further decadence. One section of the Syrian church in India accepted the authority of Rome, while the other, which remained true to Antioch, reformed and purified itself.[9]

Notices from other sources during the medieval period are also of interest, but a few more words about Marco Polo's visit may not be inappropriate here. Marco Polo visited India on his way to China at the end of the thirteenth century.

> He visited the place near Madras where the body of Thomas was supposed to lie buried. He records that the place, though of no importance commercially, was visited by pilgrims, both Christian and Muslim, and that the Christians living there supported themselves by cultivating the coconut palm. He travelled as far as Quilon, where he also found a small number of Christians.[10]

---

8. A.L. Basham, op. cit., p. 343.
9. Ibid.
10. Stephen Neill, op. cit., p. 21.

Another traveller to stop in India on way to China towards the end of the thirteenth century was John of Monte Corvino, whom the Pope had dispatched to the great Khan. He spent thirteen months in India.

> It is unfortunate that only three letters in which he has anything to tell about India have been preserved. He too had visited the Church of Thomas Christians and while there had baptized about one hundred persons. He does not tell us who these people were, whether members of the Church who in the absence of priests had never been able to be baptized, converts form Hinduism, or Nestorians, whom he regarded as not having been properly baptized.[11]

Thomas Christians in India

One way of reviewing the history of Christianity in India would be to trace the fortunes of the so-called Thomas Christians in India. We saw earlier how the Thomas Christians trace themselves to the ministry of St. Thomas in India. According to *The Acts of Judas Thomas*, an apocryphal work assigned to the second or third century:

> the Apostles who were together in Jerusalem after the Ascension of Christ, cast lots to decide where each should go to preach the Gospel. India fell to the lot of Thomas who was unwilling to go. "I have not strength enough for this, for I am weak," he protested, adding, "and I am a Hebrew, how can I teach the Indians?" Even when Jesus appeared to him in a vision he refused saying, "Whithersoever Thou wilt, O Lord, send me, only to India I will not go." As it happened, however, he was purchased as a slave by an Indian merchant and was taken to India anyway. Master and slave probably reached Taxila by the well-known sea-route from Alexandria to the mouth of the Indus, and here

11. Stephen Neill, op. cit., pp. 21-22.

> Thomas was sold once more, this time to Gudnaphar (Gondophernes) as a master-carpenter. Legend says that he succeeded in converting the king and his brother, and was allowed to preach the Gospel in the kingdom, where his simple life and abundant faith greatly impressed the people, many of whom were converted.[12]

Benjamin Walker blends legend and history when he goes on to say:

> His missionary activities in the north-west were cut short by the Kushan invasion, and he retraced his steps to the mouth of the Indus and thence took boat to Malabar, landing in the year CE 52 at the port of Muziris (Cranganore), a Roman colony near Cochin. Here too he made many converts and established churches at Palur, Cranganore, Parur, Gokkamangalam, Chayal, Niranam and Quilon. Tradition has it that he went over to the east coast of India, met with much success there and converted the local king, who was publicly baptized. He then travelled farther afield, even to China, returned to the east coast of India and was martyred by the Brahmins in CE 72. The place of his martyrdom is traditionally held to have been Mylapore, near Madras, and here he was buried. In the third century, according to one version, his remains were exhumed, carried to Edessa, and once more in the thirteenth century exhumed and taken to Ortona in Italy where they are believed to rest today.[13]

It is clear from the evidence provided by Cosmas Indicopleustes, who visited India between CE 525 and 530 that a Christian community existed in Sri Lanka and Male (Mālābār?). "The links of these remote Christians were with the patriarch of Babylon, and this means that although their

---

12. Benjamin Walker, *The Hindu World* (New York and Washington: Frederick A. Praeger, 1968), vol. I, p. 238.
13. Ibid.

descendants claim to have maintained the faith unadulterated as transmitted to them by Thomas, they were in fact, according to Western textbooks, affiliated with the Nestorian heresy."[14] The evidence provided by Marco Polo towards the end of the thirteenth century confirms their continued existence, as he "saw the tomb of St Thomas, and remarked on its popularity as a place of pilgrimage."[15] The existence of the community around the same time is also confirmed by John of Monte Corvino who "visited the Church of Thomas Christians."[16] In the next century a French Dominican, popularly known as brother Jordan, around 1321 speaks of "a scattered people, one here, another there, who call themselves Christians but are not so, nor do they have baptism, nor do they know anything about the faith; nay, they believe St Thomas the Great to be Christ."[17] The Thomas Christians are next noticed by John de Marignolli who "tells us that on Palm Sunday, 1348, he and his companions arrived at a very noble city of India called Quilon, where the whole world's pepper is produced. And the Saracens (Muslims) were not the proprietors of the trade but the Thomas Christians."[18]

The future of the Thomas Christians was however about to be influenced by developments in Europe which impinged on India. The religious context changed forever after the arrival of Vasco da Gama from Portugal in 1498.

---

14. Stephen Neill, op. cit., p. 18.
15. A.L. Basham, op. cit., p. 343.
16. Stephen Neill, op. cit., p. 22.
17. Ibid., p. 23.
18. Ibid.

Once Portuguese power had been established in India, it turned out that the "Portuguese strong point at Cochin was in the close neighbourhood of Angamalle, one of the chief centres of the Thomas Christians; and the whole of the Serra (mountains) through which they were scattered was easily accessible to European visitors. Both parties were delighted with the discovery."[19] The size of the Christian community is given as consisting of "30,000 families; and they could put in the field 30,000 armed men."[20]

The delight at mutual discovery was however short-lived. The Thomas Christians, may have "assimilated Hindu ways . . . in many points but they had scrupulously avoided the use of images, this being one of their safeguards against absorption into an idolatrous society."[21] The Roman Catholics from Portugal, however, were accustomed to using statues, which appalled the Thomas Christians. On their part, the Portuguese accused them of the Nestorian heresy they had never heard of. Moreover, the Thomas Christians were ecclesiastically connected with Mesopotamia rather than Rome.

Matters came to a head in 1599. Aleixo de Menezes was the Archbishop of Goa. When the "one remaining Syrian bishop, Mar Abraham," died in 1598 he came down to Serra "to put his carefully laid plans into execution."[22] He had the support of the Jesuits who had been running a seminary at Vaipicotta. The Portuguese presence in Cochin

19. Stephen Neill, op. cit., p. 33.

20. Ibid., p. 34.

21. Ibid.

22. Ibid., p. 35.

also helped his plans along. The events which followed may be summarized as follows:

> Menezes next proceeded to summon a synod of the entire church. On June 20, 1599, 153 priests and 660 lay representatives met at Udiyampērūr (Diamper). It was clear that the Christians had not been called to discuss, but to obey. Decrees for the reform of the church, some of them necessary and salutary, others intended simply to replace local by Roman customs, had been carefully prepared ahead of time, and were read out day by day to the assembled throng. By June 26 all was over; the decrees had been accepted in their entirety, and were signed by all present, starting with Menezes himself. The ancient Church of the Thomas Christians, as an independent church, had simply ceased to exist.[23]

The Thomas Christians however found the new arrangement too heavy-handed and yearned for an Eastern bishop.

The conflict continued for a while and "at the end of a period of twenty years it was found that about two-thirds of the people has remained within the Roman allegiance; one-third stood by the archdeacon and had organized themselves as the independent Malankara Church, faithful to the old Eastern traditions and hostile to all the Roman claims. In all of the subsequent period the lines of division have hardly changed, and things remain much as they were three centuries ago."[24]

The arrival of the Portuguese in India had signalled a change in global power equations, which culminated in

---

23. Stephen Neill, op. cit., p. 35.

24. Ibid., pp. 36-37.

the establishment of British rule over India during the next few centuries. As a result the state of Travancore, where the Thomas Christians were largely located, came under British control. Colonel Munro, who became the resident early in the nineteenth century, was "a man of strong Christian convictions . . . [who] suggested to the Christian missionary society that a mission of help should be sent, not to turn the Syrians into Anglicans, but to help in the training of the ministry and in the education of the people."[25] The idea was to help Thomas Christians get rid of the "superstitions" which had become prevalent as a result of Roman Catholic influence. The choice of the Anglican body — Church Missionary Society — is significant, for it tends to confirm the observation that the British government, at this stage of the game, "though neutral between Hindus and Muslims, always tended to treat the Church of England in India as the state Church."[26]

The delicacy of the arrangement needs to be borne in mind. Members of the Anglican Church were under strict orders not to proselytize as they cooperated with the head of the Thomas Christians — Metropolitan Dionysius III. "Up to this point the services had all been carried out in Syriac, hardly a word of which was intelligible to the people. . . . The missionaries succeeded in translating the whole Bible into Malayalam."[27] The Anglican presence however was felt by the Thomas Christians for although "the missionaries worshipped among themselves in the

25. Stephen Neill, op. cit., p. 82.

26. Ibid., p. 86.

27. Ibid., p. 83.

Anglican fashion — they were not communicants of the Syrian Church."[28] The communicants of the Syrian Church were impressed by the example set by the Anglican presence and began to agitate for changes within their Church. The younger Anglican missionaries also became less prudent in their criticism of "superstitious" Syrian practices. The break came in 1836 when contact with the Syrian Church on the part of the Anglicans was brought to a close, with a small minority seceding to the Church of England.

The momentum for reform however continued, led by Abraham Malpan, who taught Syriac at the seminary at Kottayam. His nephew, after visiting the Syrian Patriarch at Mardin in Syria, returned in 1843 as "bishop and metran for the Syrian Church." By 1865, however, a rival party had Pulikot Joseph consecrated as metran.

> This led to fourteen years of bitter disputes between Matthew and Dionysius V, as Pulikot Joseph now styled himself. A personal visit of the Patriarch to India from 1875 to 1877 immensely strengthened the hands of Dionysius and the conservative party, and also established a domination of the Patriarch over the church such as had never been known before. The death of Matthew in 1877 did not clear up the situation, since his successor, Mar Thomas Athanasius, had already been consecrated.[29]

Matters came to a head in 1879 when Thomas Athanasius lost the legal battle. This led to the formation of yet another Church and the Mar Thoma Syrian Church came into being. With a membership of about 200,000, it was considerably smaller than either the Roman Catholic or Malankara

---

28. Stephen Neill, op. cit., p. 83.
29. Ibid., p. 107.

sections of the Church. Stephen Neill goes on to point out however that

> the division of the two parties into two churches did not bring peace to the conservatives. Their unity was threatened by deep-seated differences of opinion as to the rights of the Patriarch and the relative independence of the Indian Church. More than two generations were to pass before this strife was healed. This section of the Church, much weakened by these contentions and a number of secessions to Rome resulting from them, has received much help from the Anglo-Catholic wing of the Anglican Church, and specially from the Oxford Mission of Calcutta.[30]

This brief account of the vicissitudes in the history of the Thomas Christians from around the third century to the present provides a useful starting point for the history of Christianity in India in general. It enables us to mark out three phases in its history in India: (1) when it was primarily represented by Thomas Christians; (2) when, after the arrival of the Portuguese towards the end of the fifteenth century, it also came to be represented by the Roman Catholics; and (3) when, with the appearance of European Protestant powers in India, another form of Christianity, namely the Protestant, came to be represented in India. We have surveyed the history of the Thomas Christians, and a brief sketch of the history of the Roman Catholics and the Protestants in India is offered in the same spirit.

Catholics in India

The conquest of Goa by the Portuguese ultimately resulted in the establishment of a Roman Catholic outpost on the Indian subcontinent. There are two versions on how this

---

30. Stephen Neill, op. cit., p. 108.

came about — the mild version and the severe version. According to the mild version:

> The Portuguese felt no strong impulse to preach the gospel to the people of India as a whole. Nor, as is often affirmed, did they exercise force to bring the local inhabitants to the Christian faith. It was, however, firmly held that idolatry must not be practised in the territories of a Christian king; if the people wished to retain their disagreeable rites, they must observe them secretly and out of sight. No doubt many inducements were held out to the Hindus with a view to securing their assent to the new faith; a non-Christian could hardly hope for employment or advancement under this Christian government. But those who accepted the Christian faith were always a minority of the inhabitants.[31]

According to the severe version the Portuguese were not above resorting to coercion as a mode of conversion.[32] The following account seems to offer a balanced picture incorporating both the elements.

> The Portuguese, crusading against the Moor in North Africa, carried with them to the East something of the same zeal and the same hostility to all Muslims. But their motives had always been mixed, and once in India those of commerce early became dominant. So, though the Portuguese Crown had been made by the Pope patron of all missions and churches in the Indies, it was not until the advent of the Jesuits in 1542 that any great missionary activity was displayed. Their influence at the Mughul court will be examined in subsequent chapters. A like effort was made by the society in China and Japan. The introduction of the Inquisition in Goa after 1560, with its cruel persecution, served only to undo much of the good work done by the

---

31. Stephen Neill, op. cit., p. 29.

32. A.K. Priolkar, *The Goa Inquisition* (New Delhi: Voice of India, 1961).

Jesuits and the Mendicant orders.[33]

Special note must be taken of the Jesuits, as members of the Society of Jesus by Ignatius Loyola (1491–1556) are commonly known. This society was founded in the sixteenth century[34] and one of its members, Francis Xavier (1506-52), was a companion of Ignatius Loyola. He has been called "one of the outstanding missionaries of all times."[35] He spent four years in India. Once matters of Goa had been taken care of he directed his attentions elsewhere, for which some historical backdrop needs to be provided.

The land stretching from the Kanya Kumari to Chennai is often referred to as the Coromandel Coast. A people usually called the Paravas, and who called themselves Bharathas, dwelt on the coastline, eking out a livelihood by fishing under the fear of pirates and marauders. Now,

> Hearing of the new power that had appeared in India, they desired to place themselves under the protection of the foreigners. Their request was granted, on the condition that they accept baptism and regard the king of Portugal as their overlord. The terms were accepted. In a brief space the entire caste, numbering perhaps ten thousand people, was baptized, without any instruction and with no provision for spiritual care; all that the people knew was that they were now called Christians. There is some doubt as to the date at which these events took place. The most probable

---

33. Percival Spear, ed., *The Oxford History of India* (4th edn.) (Delhi: Oxford University Press, 1994), p. 330.

34. Willard G. Oxtoby, "The Christian Tradition", in Willard G. Oxtoby ed., *Worlds Religions: Western Traditions* (Toronto: Oxford University Press, 1996), pp. 299-301.

35. Stephen Neill, op. cit., p. 30.

date seems to be 1536, or six years before the arrival of Xavier in Goa. During these years nothing had been done for these people, except that the strong arm of Portuguese protection had made it possible for them to live.[36]

Francis Xavier now turned his attention to these people. He has provided a vivid picture of his work among these people.

> On Sunday I assemble all the people, men and women, young and old. . . . I give out the first commandment, which they repeat, and then we say all together, "Jesus Christ, Son of God, grant us grace to love thee above all things." When we have asked for this grace, we recite the Paternoster together, and then cry with one accord, "Holy Mary, Mother of Jesus Christ, obtain for us grace from thy Son to enable us to keep the first commandment . . ." and so on through all the other commandments.[37]

Xavier's mission was a great success, so much so that

> By the end of the sixteenth century the Jesuits had succeeded in gathering the Christians together in sixteen large villages, in each of which a Jesuit priest was resident. The priest exercised a wide-reaching and paternal authority over every part of the life of the people. It was a strict rule that there must be no fishing on Sunday, and that part of ever Friday's catch must be handed over for the support of the church. Little was done for education, and as in Portugal itself the greater part of the population remained illiterate. But gradually the life and mind of the people came to be saturated with the Roman Catholic tradition as it had developed in the days after the Council of Trent. The Fisher Coast is still an almost entirely Roman Catholic country.[38]

---

36. Stephen Neill, op. cit., pp. 30-31.
37. Ibid., p. 32.
38. Ibid., p. 32-33.

Apart from the Goa and the Coromandel Coast, the Roman Catholics also gained a footing in Kerala under circumstances which have been described earlier.

Two other dimensions of the Jesuit presence in India are worth noting. The Jesuits were in touch with Akbar and participated in the debates on religion arranged by him, at one point even hoping for the conversion of Akbar. More significant from the point of view of both Christianity and Hinduism was the experiment undertaken by the Jesuit Robert de Nobili (d. 1656). Until his arrival, the Portuguese policy was to Europeanize all Christian converts who were mainly drawn from the lower classes, as illustrated by the case of the Paravas. Robert de Nobili wanted to change this state of affairs. He adopted the lifestyle of a *brāhmaṇa* and sought converts form the higher castes while living at Madurai and "it appears that in point of fact about 600 persons of the higher castes had been baptized in thirty-seven years,"[39] although not all of them may have remained faithful.[40] Robert de Nobili was criticized for adopting these methods and defended himself but gradually his methods fell into disfavour. Robert de Nobili had even introduced Indian ingredients in Christian ritual but

> In 1744 the Pope again took action to settle forever the question of the Malabar rites; no further dispensations could be permitted, and from now on the Christianity of India was to reflect in every detail the Christianity of Rome. Robert de Nobili's principle of "accommodation," the will to disrupt as little as possible the life and customs of the converts, was utterly rejected. Nearly two centuries were to pass before

---

39. Stephen Neill, op. cit., p. 39.

40. Ibid.

> the official world of the Roman Catholic Church was again to take seriously the idea that Christianity need not necessarily be absolutely uniform in all the countries of the world.[41]

It has been calculated by the year 1750 "there were roughly a million Christians in India, about one half in Goa and the other Portuguese possessions, a quarter in Kerala, the home of the Thomas Christians, and the remainder scattered throughout the rest of the country."[42]

Protestants in India

By now however Protestant missionaries had begun to appear on the scene. They even tried to carry out their missionary activity among the Roman Catholics in India. It is recorded that when the Dutch Protestant Phillipus Baldeus attempted to convert some of the Parava Christians they replied:

> Our great apostle Francis Xavier vindicated the truth of his Gospel by raising several people from the dead. If you will be good enough to follow his example, we shall be happy to pay attention to your words.[43]

Protestant missions were more successful elsewhere. The Danish Protestant mission was successful in converting a large number of Nādārs in the area of Cape Comorin or Kanya Kumari — the tip of India — towards the beginning of the nineteenth century. The Nādārs

> made their living by climbing the palmyra tree to draw from it the sweet juice which is the local substitute for sugar. The

41. Stephen Neill, op. cit., p. 45.
42. Ibid., p. 47.
43. Ibid., p. 52.

> Nādārs, a rough and vigorous people, who have shown a remarkable capacity for development under the influence of education, were not untouchable, but had no access to Hindu temples. It was perhaps their ambiguous status that made them so readily accessible to the Christian gospel. Between May 30, 1800, and June 24, 1803, the Lutheran missionaries baptized 5,670 of these people. It is not clear what amount of preparation had been given them, or what provision was made for their care afterwards. The whole district was left in the charge of Satyanathan, one of the most faithful and gifted of the Indian pastors. In this remote and obscure corner of the world the foundations of a living church had been laid.[44]

The missionary Schwartz had been instrumental in bringing about these conversions and his work was continued by Hough and then Rhenius. By the time Rhenius died in 1838 "there were Christian groups in nearly three hundred villages over an area of 2,000 square miles."[45]

The other area in which the Protestant missionary movements have been successful is in the tribal areas such as Chotanagpur in the tribal belt in central India. It is worth noting that Roman Catholics had already been active in the area and that "the Roman Catholic Church still has in the area a larger number of Christians than the Anglicans and the Lutherans combined."[46] The Jesuits had been active in the area among them. Protestant missions have been active among the Gonds and Bhils. Other tribal peoples among whom Protestant Christian missions have been successful are the Santhals on the border of Bengal and

---

44. Stephen Neill, op. cit., p. 61.
45. Ibid.
46. Ibid., p. 101.

Bihar, the Khonds in Orissa, and the Khasis and the Nagas in the North-East, and, to a limited extent, among the Todas in the Nilgiris.

Similar missions among untouchable communities in India have also met with success, as among the Mālas and the Maḍigas in Andra Pradesh, and among the Chuhrā community in Punjab.

Stephen Neill presents a thumbnail sketch of Christianity in India in 1914 as follows:

> It seems that in 1914 the Christians in the whole of India numbered about three and a half million. Of these nearly two-thirds were Roman Catholic, 10 per cent Christians of the independent Syrian churches, and about a quarter Protestant. The Roman Catholics had quadrupled their number in a century. Proportionately the progress of the Protestants had been much more rapid; since starting from almost nothing at the beginning of the nineteenth century, they had multiplied themselves eight times over in the years between 1858 and 1914. Christians were, however, very unevenly distributed. In some areas of the south they were so numerous as to produce in the mind of a visitor almost the impression of being in a Christian country. In many areas Christians were a tiny minority. In yet others nothing had been done at all, either because, as in Rewa, one of the larger Indian native states, the Hindu ruler forbade all Christian propaganda in his area, or because the always slender Christian forces had not found it possible to penetrate so far.[47]

The next phase of the Christian presence in India coincides with the rise of the independence movement in which may Christians participated. Some issues within the Christian

47. Stephen Neill, op. cit., pp. 111-12.

community are also worth noting, before one turns to its relationship to the other religious communities in India. One major problem was caused by the presence of numerous denominations. As Stephen Neill graphically puts it: "If five or six different missions are working in one place, any non-Christian who wishes to become a Christian is faced with a cruel dilemma: To which of the Christian bodies should he give his allegiance?"[48] The problem however is not as acute as it used to be earlier. The various Protestant denominations came together to constitute the Church of South India in 1947, but the severity of the problem can be recognized in the following fact:

> An outstanding leader of the Congregationalist Church, C.J. Lucas, has left it on record that his father was a Lutheran, his mother a Congregationalist, his wife an Anglican, one son in the South India United Church, another confirmed as an Anglican Bishop, one brother-in-law a Methodist, and several other relatives Roman Catholics.[49]

The question of the emergence of an Indian Christian leadership used to be an issue during the British period and has by and large been resolved now. An issue which still remains unresolved is the degree to which the Christian Church should accommodate itself to Hindu culture. The following historical background is helpful here:

> Christians have at different times taken up various attitudes towards non-Christian religions. In early days the view of most missionaries was entirely negative: these religions are simply the invention of the devil to deceive men and lead them away from the heavenly Father. From about 1875

48. Stephen Neill, op. cit., p. 147.

49. Ibid., p. 148.

> onwards this severe attitude began to change, and to be replaced by interest in, and sometimes an enthusiastic respect for, the ancient Asian forms of wisdom. In all except very conservative circles, it is accepted generally by Christians in India and Pakistan that they should know their own languages well and correct the tendency towards a Christian jargon which was marked in the nineteenth century, that they must be interested in the traditional culture of the country, and that they must try to enter with sympathy into the experiences of their non-Christian fellow citizens.[50]

It might be worth adding that the spread of Christianity in India was not entirely free from violence, though largely so. Four Dominicans, for instance, ran afoul of the Muslim regime and met their end in the following way in 1321:

> A French Dominican, Jourdain Catalini de Séverac, commonly known as Brother Jordan, was travelling in the company of four Franciscans. They landed on the island of Salsette, and there found fifteen families of Nestorian Christians. Jordan crossed to the mainland, leaving the Franciscans at Salsette. During his absence, three of the friars were called before the *Cadi*, the Muslim judge, in connection with a case which had nothing to do with religion. In the course of the inquiry, the judge began to ask them questions about their religion, and at a certain point pressed them for their opinion of Muhammad. One of the brothers, truthfully but imprudently, replied that it was his opinion that Muhammad was the son of perdition and that he was now in hell where the adherents of his religion would follow him in due course. Naturally the fanatical Muslims were enraged. The brothers were tortured and then deported to the mainland, but during the following night they were pursued by armed men and put to death. The one remaining friar was also arrested, tortured and finally beheaded. Jordan

50. Stephen Neill, op. cit., p. 165.

> heard the news some days later, returned to Salsette, and was allowed to collect the remains of the martyrs and to carry them to a place named Sefa, where there was also a church, for safe Christian burial.[51]

John D. Britto, who visiting India from Brazil, also lost his life under unfortunate circumstances.

> De Britto's special concern was with the Christians in the area now known as Ramnad. For seven years the opposition of the local ruler had made it impossible for any Jesuit to visit the scattered Christians. De Britto's first visit, in 1686, ended in imprisonment and torture, but in the end he and his companions were set free by the local ruler. With undiminished confidence de Britto attempted a second visit in 1693; this time no release was made; the Jesuit was beheaded outside the little town of Uraiyur, leaving behind the memory of a singularly guileless and gentle personality and of total devotion to the cause of Christ.[52]

Christianity After Independence

The arrival of Indian independence changed the political contours of the country but not the religious. The proportion of Indian population which is Christian is often placed at three per cent. It was largely concentrated in Kerala and Goa but has also become a major presence in the north-east as in the post-independent India. It has been roughly estimated that fifty per cent of Indian Christians are Roman Catholics, and that half or more than two-thirds of all Indian Christians are of Dalit or tribal origin.[53]

---

51. Stephen Neill, op. cit., p. 22.
52. Ibid., p. 40.
53. Robert Eric Frykenberg, *Christianity in India: from Beginnings to the Present* (New York: Oxford University Press, 2005), p. 464.

At the moment the Christian scene is undergoing some changes. A category of crypto-Christians has been identified, who have converted to Christianity but overlook the fact for the sake benefiting from the pro-Dalit policies of the government (for which only Hindu Dalits are strictly eligible).[54] Christian proselytization has picked up speed in recent years, especially through the presence of the Pentecostal movement in India. More than one scholar has pointed out that the Christian population of India should be more realistically estimated at around seven percent.[55]

---

54. Donald Eugene Smith, *India as a Secular State* (Princeton: Princeton University Press, 1963), pp. 322-23.

55. Robert Eric Frykenberg, op. cit., p. 464.

7

Must "Christianity" Proselytize?

I

CHRISTIAN proselytization has been a sore point with many Hindus. The following conversation between C.F. Andrews and Mahatma Gandhi goes to the heart of the issue:

> ***C.F. Andrews:*** What would you say to a man who after considerable thought and prayer said that he could not have his peace and salvation except by becoming a Christian?
>
> ***Gandhiji:*** I would say if a non-Christian (say a Hindu) came to a Christian and made that statement, he should ask him to become a good Hindu rather than find goodness in change of faith.
>
> ***C.F.A.:*** I cannot in this go the whole length with you, though you know my own position. I discarded the position that there is no salvation except through Christ long ago. But supposing the Oxford Group Movement people changed the life of your son, and he felt like being converted, what would you say?
>
> ***Gandhiji:*** I would say that the Oxford Group may change the lives of as many as they like, but not their religion. They can draw their attention to the best in their respective religions and change their lives by asking them to live according to them. There came to me a man, the son of brahmana parents, who said his reading of your book had

led him to embrace Christianity. I asked him if he thought that the religion of his forefathers was wrong. He said, "No." Then I said: "Is there any difficulty about your accepting the Bible as one of the great religious books of the world and Christ as one of the great teachers?" I said to him that you had never through your books asked Indians to take up the Bible and embrace Christianity, and that he had misread your book — unless of course your position is like that of the late M. Mahomed Ali's, viz. that "a believing Mussulman, however bad his life, is better than a good Hindu."

C.F.A.: I do not accept M. Mahomed Ali's position at all. But I do say that if a person really needs a change of faith I should not stand in his way.

Gandhiji: But don't you see that you do not even give him a chance? You do not even cross-examine him. Supposing a Christian came to me and said he was captivated by a reading of the *Bhagavata* and so wanted to declare himself a Hindu, I should say to him: "No. What the *Bhagavata* offers the Bible also offers. You have not yet made the attempt to find it out. Make the attempt and be a good Christian."

C.F.A.: I don't know. If someone earnestly says that he will become a good Christian, I should say, "You may become one," though you know that I have in my own life strongly dissuaded ardent enthusiasts who came to me. I said to them, "Certainly not on *my* account will you do anything of the kind." But human nature does require a concrete faith.

Gandhiji: If a person wants to believe in the Bible let him say so, but why should he discard his own religion? This proselytization will mean no peace in the world. Religion is a very personal matter. We should by living the life according to our lights share the best with one another, thus adding to the sum total of human effort to reach God.

"Consider," continued Gandhiji, "whether you are going to accept the position of mutual toleration or of equality of all religions. My position is that all the great religions are fundamentally equal. We must have innate respect for other religions as we have for our own. Mind you, not mutual toleration, but equal respect."[1]

II

Although in the course of this conversation C.F. Andrews reveals himself as a liberal Christian, the attitude of Christianity towards India has been largely evangelical. Any presentation of Christianity meant for the Hindus must go into the matter in some depth. One must thus examine the evidence on which the Christian sense of mission is based. As a Hindu, one would also like to know whether there is any scope for toning down this proselytizing zeal within Christianity. For otherwise the Hindu is only left with the option of countering this Christian proselytizing zeal with one of his or her own, which can lead to violent outcomes.[2]

The foundational text for Christians is the New Testament. There are three passages in the New Testament which have typically been utilized by Christians to establish that Christians are under a religious obligation to proselytize. The four Gospels of the New Testament provide accounts of the life of Jesus and three of them are often referred to as the "synoptic" gospels on account of their similarities. One of these synoptic gospels, that of Matthew, contains the following passage:

---

1. Mahatma Gandhi, *Hindu Dharma* (Ahmedabad: Navajivan Press, 1958), pp. 230-32.
2. See *India Today International*, 6 October, 2003, p. 24 on the murder of Graham Staines.

> *Go therefore and make disciples of all nations, baptizing them in the name of the Father, and of the Son, and of the Holy Spirit.* — Matthew 28:19

This clearly seems a call to go out and proselytize.

Similarly, the fourth Gospel, that of John, also contains the following statement:

> *I am the way, the truth, and the life: no one comes to the Father except through me.* — John 14:6

The force of this passage is increased if one recognizes the following general fact about the nature of this gospel:

> Repeatedly throughout John's gospel, Jesus declares himself in passages that begin with "I am," making claims to be the means of salvation. In chapter 6: "I am the bread of life; he who comes to me shall not hunger, and he who believes in me shall never thirst." In chapter 8: "I am the light of the world; he who follows me will not walk in darkness, but will have the light of life." In chapter 10: "I am the good shepherd. The good shepherd lays down his life for the sheep." In chapter 11: "I am the resurrection and the life; he who believes in me, though he die, yet shall he live, and whoever lives and believes in me shall never die." In chapter 14: "I am the way, and the truth, and the life; no one comes to the Father, but by me." In chapter 15: "I am the vine, you are the branches. He who abides in me, and I in him, he it is that bears much fruit, for apart from me you can do nothing." John's Jesus is more than a teacher with an insight into human nature; he is presented as the definitive link between God and humanity.[3]

The Gospels are followed by the Acts, wherein the early Christian community has the stirring experience of the Holy Spirit. Therein too one finds the following statement:

---

3. Willard Oxtoby, op. cit., p. 211.

> *For there is no other name under Heaven given among human beings, whereby we must be saved.* — Acts 4:12

This statement should be viewed in the context provided by the following passage:

> Various explanations are offered for how the early Church transformed its identity from a Jewish sect to an independent missionary religion. In the New Testament book *Acts of the Apostles*, a sequel to his gospel, Luke presents the mandate in miraculous terms, as one might expect him to. In *Acts* 2 the disciples are gathered on Shavuoth, the festival seven weeks after the Passover on which Jesus was executed. They experience the Holy Spirit as a rush of wind and fire, and begin to speak — and be understood — in diverse languages, thus enabled to preach to all people.[4]

Professor Krister Stendahl examines this passage and begins by remarking:

> I have an old exegetical rule which says that when you apply the right answer to the wrong question, it will always be wrong, even if — or especially if — the answer is God's word. Now what was the question to which Peter gave that answer in Acts?[5]

He goes on to say:

> The question was the accusation, the accusation that Peter had performed the miracle of a magician in his own name and he answers by the exclamation: "Heavens no, in no other name is there salvation but Jesus." This does not relate to the problem of Christianity and Buddhism — at least not on the conscious level. But words like that grow legs and walk out of their context.[6]

---

4. Willard Oxtoby, op. cit., p. 212.

5. Krister Stendahl, "From God's Perspective We are All Minorities", *The Journal of Religious Pluralism* (1993), p. 3.

6. Ibid.

He also makes a more general point in the light of which the statement might be revisited. For he goes on to say:

> And even when that is legitimate we must also remind ourselves of the very nature of confessional language. As Eastern Christianity has always known better than the West, confessional language is doxological. It is a way of praising God. It is the primary language of faith. The home language of the Church is the language of prayer, worship and doxology, giving praise out of the fullness of one's heart. Actually, confessional and liturgical and doxological language is a kind of caressing language by which we express our devotion with abandon and joy. Raymond Brown, the outstanding Roman Catholic exegete, in writing about the development of Biblical studies in the Roman Catholic Church, hails Pius the XII's encyclical of 1943, long before Vatican II, as the milestone in setting Biblical scholarship free in Catholic studies. This the encyclical did when it admitted or even hailed the fact that in studying scriptures you have to study the genre, the style, the nature of the language it has, so that you don't read it in the wrong key. I think this is apropos to Acts 4:12. I can preach wonderful sermons on this but I have to restrict myself.[7]

Although the passages as they stand clearly make Christianity appear as a proselytizing religion, some scholars have argued that if the passages are examined closely such a judgement will have to be reassessed.

Thus it has been pointed out in relation to the passage in Matthew that in this gospel "as a writer, Matthew is clearly addressing a Jewish audience,"[8] and "presumes that for his readers, the Hebrew scriptures have a literal, textual

---

7. Krister Stendahl, op. cit., pp. 4-5.
8. Willard Oxtoby, op. cit., p. 207.

authority."[9] This fact has a crucial bearing on the interpretation of the passage involved. Krister Stendahl writes:

> Anyone who reads Matthew's gospel finds this a rather stunning statement towards the end, because Matthew's gospel is totally built on the theory that during the ministry of Jesus, neither Jesus nor the disciples were to move outside Israel. Matthew has rather striking statements: "Do not go to any Gentiles. . . . You will not lack cities in Israel before the Son of Man appears" (10:5 and 23). This concentration on the mission to Israel has its contrast in the announcement of the Gentile mission in the last verses of the Gospel — "all the nations" refers to "all the Gentiles." But what kind of a mission is this? How did Matthew — if we stay on that level — think of this mission? Did he think of it as a saturation mission, did he think of it as the christianization of the world, the cosmos?
>
> I think we can be very clear that Matthew thinks of the mission of the Church on a minority model, as did Paul. You will remember that in Romans 15 Paul says, "I have a principle: never run a mission where anybody else has preached the gospel before. And now I have run out of space, there is no place for me to go in the East. So I have to go to Spain, I have to go West." That's an odd way of looking at things. What matters to Paul seems to be establishing a presence, a small minority in these centres of the East. It is a minority image, it is the establishment, as I like to say, of Laboratory II. Israel was Laboratory I, and when God felt that some good things had been achieved in Laboratory I, God said "Let's now try it out on a somewhat broader basis . . . on a Gentile basis"; but still a laboratory with Christians as the guinea pigs, Christians as another "peculiar people."

---

9. Willard Oxtoby, op. cit., p. 207.

> The images in the gospel of Matthew are minority images. "You are the salt of the earth." Nobody wants the world to be a salt mine. "You are the light of the world and let your light so shine before the people that they see your good deeds and become Christians." *That's not what it says.* It says: that they see your good deeds and praise your Father who is in Heaven, have some reason for joy, that's what it says.[10]

In other words, it can be argued that the followers of Jesus went much further with the claims than might have been intended.

The passage in John also is capable of a revised reading. Jesus certainly believed himself to be in a unique relationship with God. However "it is important to notice that he is not represented as preaching publicly on this theme, but as only occasionally of it within the confined circle of his closest friends and followers."[11] This leads one to believe that Jesus' experience in this respect was too intimate and intense to be meant for public consumption. It has been pointed out that in the prayer in the garden at Gethsemane (*Mark* XIV.36) God is addressed as the intimate *Ăbbā* rather than the more formal *Ābhi* and further that the almost divine self-confidence with which he preached, claiming to supersede the Old testament teaching (*Matthew* V.21 f); or reject oral tradition (*Mark* VII, 6-9) to say nothing of interfering with Temple affairs is difficult to account for "except on the basis of that assurance of Sonship which

10. Krister Stendahl, "From God's Perspective We Are All Minorities," *The Journal of Religious Pluralism* (1992) II:5.

11. J.G. Davies, "Christianity: The Early Church", in R.C. Zaehner, ed., *The Concise Encyclopedia of Living Faiths* (Boston: Beacon Press, 1967), p. 53.

the writers of the first three (synoptic) gospels associated with his baptism: 'Thou art my beloved Son' (*Mark* I, ii; cf. ix.7)."[12] J.G. Davies goes on to say:

> In the light of these considerations, we may accept the statement of his Sonship, ascribed to Jesus in *Matthew* xi, 27 and *Luke* x, 22 as consistent with what we have seen above to be Jesus' own conception: "All things have been delivered unto me of my Father; and no one knoweth the Son, save the Father; neither doth any know the Father, save the Son, and he to whomsoever the Son willeth to reveal him." Jesus thus believed himself to stand in a unique filial relationship to God.[13]

In the light of these facts the passage from the gospel of John utilized to justify proselytization assumes a very different character. It appears to be more like a personal communication than a public commission. As Krister Stendahl notes:

> The Johannine passage is found in the beginning of what is called the farewell speech of Jesus. The setting is this: "Do not be upset in your hearts, believe in God, believe also in me. I'm going to leave you, but in this world there are many ways — many ways — for you to stay. If there were not I would take you with me right now, but you can stay here. Don't' worry. . . . And you know the way to where I am going." Then Thomas asks: "But we don't know where you are going. How can we then know the way?" Thomas is always pretty smart, good questions, good logic. Jesus said to him: "I am the way, the truth and the life. Nobody comes to the Father except through me."
>
> It strikes me very old to take a passage from the most intimate and tender conversation with the most intimate and closest

12. J.G. Davies, op. cit., .
13. J.G. Davies, op. cit., p. 54.

circle of disciples, from a context in which their hearts are full of foreboding with the imminent fear of relations about to be severed, to lift a word from *that* conversation, and use it in answering the question of Christianity's relation to other religions. It is just not apropos. It is odd that one of the few passages that are used by those who have closed the doors on a theology of religions in Christianity, should be a passage which is dealing not with the question of the periphery or the margins of exclusion, but which, on the contrary, lies at the very heart of the mystery of what came to be the Trinity: the relation between the Father and the Son.[14]

III

The point then is the situation is not as hopeless as the Hindu might be initially led to assume. Christianity does possess a missionary imperative but the actual shape it assumes in the field involves a consideration of several parameters which operate within Christian missiology itself. The issue may be formulated as follows:

> How, in the wider *mission dei,* are we to define *mission Christi* and the *mission ecclesia*, to use the terms which Catholic theologians have used to cope with this problem.[15]

Once the issue is framed in this way many possibilities emerge. For the mission of God (*missio dei*) may be broader in scope than the mission of Christ (*missio Christi*) and the mission of Christ — as cosmic Christ for instance — may be broader than the mission of the Church (*missio ecclesia*).

14. Krister Stendahl, op. cit., p. 4.

15. Ibid., p. 2.

IV

One unfortunate consequence of evangelical enthusiasm is the tendency on the part of Christians to depict other religions as inferior to Christianity. Such a negative portrayal of Hinduism is naturally resented by the Hindus and may even make them feel resentful of Christianity.

It is important to hear other voices within Christianity on this point also. We saw above how Christian scholars have themselves produced arguments which act as an antidote to what the Hindu might be disposed to describe as proselytizing poison. Similarly, other Christian scholars have pointed out that those Christians who misrepresent a religion are guilty of breaking one of the Ten Commandments by which they swear — namely, that one shall not bear false witness.

Bibliography

Basham, A.L., *The Wonder That Was India* (New Delhi: Rupa & Co., 1999).

Buitenen, J.A.B. van, *Tales of Ancient India*, Chicago: The University of Chicago Press, 1959.

Ch'en, Kenneth K.S., *Buddhism: The Light of Asia*, Haupagge, N.Y.: Barrons' Educational Series, 1968.

Davies, J.G., "Christianity: The Early Church", in R.C. Zaehner, ed., *The Concise Encyclopedia of Living Faiths*, Boston: Beacon Press, 1967.

Durant, Will, *Our Oriental Heritage*, New York: Simon and Schuster, 1954.

Fieser, James and John Powers, *Scriptures of the West*, 2nd edn., New York: McGraw Hill, 2004.

Fischer, Mary Pat, *Living Religions*, 3rd edn., Upper Saddle River, N.J.: Prentice Hall, 1997.

Frykenberg, Robert Eric, *Christianity in India: From Beginnings to the Present*, New York: Oxford University Press, 2008.

Gandhi, M.K., *Hindu Dharma*, Ahmedabad: Navajivan Press, 1958.

———, *Gandhi's Autobiography: The Story of My Experiments with Truth* tr. Mahadev Desai, Washington, D.C.: Public Affairs Press, 1940.

Godman, David, ed., *The Teachings of Sri Ramana Maharshi*, London and New York: Arkana, 1985.

Halbfass, Wilhelm, *India and Europe: An Essay in Understanding*, Albany, N.Y.: State University of New York Press, 1988.

Hay, Stephen, ed., *Sources of Indian Tradition*, 2nd edn., New York: Columbia University Press, 1988, vol II.

Hick, John H., *Philosophy of Religion*, 4th edn., Englewood Cliffs, New Jersey: Prentice Hall, 1990.

India Today International, 6 October, 2003.

Ludwig, Theodore M., *The Sacred Paths*, Upper Saddle Rive, New Jersey: Prentice Hall, 2001.

Majumdar, R.C., ed., *The Age of Imperial Unity*, Bombay: Bharatiya Vidya Bhavan, 1968.

Nag, Kalidas and Debajyoti Burman, eds., *The English Works of Raja Rammohun Roy*, Calcutta: Sadharan Brahmo Samaj, 1947.

Neill, Stephen, *The Story of the Christian Church in India and Pakistan*, Grand Rapids, Michigan: William B. Eerdmans Publishing Company, 1970.

Oegema, Gerbern S., *The Anointed and His People*, Sheffield: Sheffield Academic Press, 1998.

Oxtoby, Willard G., "The Christian Tradition", in Willard G. Oxtoby, ed., *World Religions: Western Traditions*, Toronto: Oxford University Press, 1996.

Renou, Louis, ed., *Hinduism*, New York: George Braziller, 1962.

Sachau, Edward C., tr., *Alberuni's India*, London: Kegan Paul, Trench, Trübner & Co., 1914, vol. II.

Sen, K.M., *Hinduism*, Harmondsworth: Penguin, 1961.

Sharma, Arvind, *Classical Hindu Thought: An Introduction*, New Delhi: Oxford University Press, 2001.

Sircar, D.C., "The Yavanas," in R.C. Majumdar, ed., *The Age of Imperial Unity*, Bombay: Bharatiya Vidya Bhavan, 1968.

Sivaramakrishna, V., "The Mahasvami as a Guide to Poetic Appreciation", in *Dilip* 30:4, October–December 2004.

Smith, Donald Eugene, *India as a Secular State*, Princeton: Princeton University Press, 1963.

Smith, Huston, *The World's Religions*, San Francisco: Harper, 1991.

Spear, Percival, ed., *The Oxford History of India*, 4th edn., Delhi: Oxford University Press, 1994.

Stark, Rodney, *The Rise of Christianity*, San-Francisco:, Harper 1997.

Stendahl, Krister, "From God's Perspective We Are All Minorities," *The Journal of Religious Pluralism*, 2:1-13 (1993).

Walker, Benjamin, *The Hindu World*, New York and Washington: Frederick A. Praeger, 1968.

Zaehner, R.C., ed., *The Concise Encyclopedia of Living Faiths*, Boston: Beacon Press, 1967.

Index